livewire JEWELRY

Make Colorful Designs
That Shine

Katie Hacker

NORTH LIGHT BOOKS

CINCINNATI, OHIO

table of contents

introduction

While my first jewelry projects were friendship pins and bracelets, my love affair with making jewelry began in earnest when I was a teenager and couldn't find cool clip earrings for my unpierced ears. Learning how to make a good basic loop was the key. Over the years, I've experimented with many different techniques, but wire wrapping is one I return to again and again. With just a few basic skills, you can make a huge variety of creative, stylish jewelry designs.

I'm not a wire purist. I love combining crystals, chain and other components with my wirework because it's the kind of jewelry I like to wear. Colored wire has gotten a bit of a bad rap in the jewelry-making world, where sterling silver wire reigns supreme. But, with the ever-rising costs of precious metals, jewelry makers need to think about economical alternatives to make stylish jewelry that won't break the bank. Plus, the metallic luster of colored wire works beautifully with crystals. And, if you get tired of a particular piece of jewelry, you won't feel bad about cutting it up to reuse the crystals. Those never go out of style!

The title of this book can be read two ways. It's *live* as in colorful and "alive," but it's also jewelry for the way you *live*. Pick the projects that speak to you and make them your own. Whether you create the projects from beginning to end or pick and choose your favorite techniques, you're going to find loads of ideas and inspiration in these pages.

katie

wire

The colorful wires that have hit jewelry supply aisles are the foundations of the designs in this book. You can create numerous design features—from dainty spiraled dangles to sturdy foundations—using this versatile material. I like using colored wire because it's easy to manipulate and offers creative design options. Of course, you can use German style plated wire, steel wire, precious metal wire or any other shaping wire to create your own versions of the projects in this book.

The projects in this book feature Artistic Wire in various colors and gauges. Artistic Wire is the most extensive line of permanently colored copper wire for jewelry and crafts. The coating is specially engineered to resist tarnishing, chipping and peeling. It can stand up to coiling, twisting, wrapping and other wire-working techniques.

When choosing a wire gauge, you have to find a balance between strength, malleability and personal preference. In general, 18-gauge wire is great for basic loops, 20-gauge wire is perfect for ear wires, 22-gauge is standard for wrapped loops and 24-gauge is useful for wrapping onto a foundation.

Spooled wire has a natural curve. Working with the curve results in smoother loops and spirals. If necessary, you can straighten spooled wire by running it through flat-nose nylon jaw pliers.

Wire comes in a range of diameters, or *gauges*. The higher the number, the smaller the gauge: 28-gauge is thinner than 18-gauge.

beads and pendants

You can get plenty of shine for your jewelry creations using beautiful colored wire, but pairing your designs with crystals guarantees a knockout look.

1 5826 curved pearl	**4** 3700 marguerite lochrose	**7** 5040 and 5041 rondelle	**10** 5203 polygon
2 5752 clover	**5** 5810 round pearl	**8** 5000 round	**11** 5500 teardrop
3 5020 helix	**6** 5301 and 5328 bicone	**9** 5523 cosmic	**12** 5601 cube

1 4139 cosmic ring   **3** 6012 flat briolette   **5** 1128 channels   **7** 6621 twist
2 4439 square ring   **4** 6656 galactic   **6** 6240 wild heart

I love sparkle, and I'm partial to *Swarovski Elements*, which are the finest precision-cut crystals in the world. These beads and pendants come in a dazzling array of shapes, sizes and colors, many of which are available to beaders under the *Create Your Style* brand. Alternatively, the projects in this book can be created with any of your favorite beads. Just keep in mind that you will need to test the project's recommended wire diameter in the holes of the substituted beads.

. . . .

stringing materials

Many books on the market explain how to make wire jewelry in detail, but not many combine wire wrapping with traditional beading techniques. I blend other stringing materials with my wirework because it's the kind of jewelry I like to wear.

FLEXIBLE BEADING WIRE (1)
Soft and strong, flexible beading wire is nylon-coated wire that is made from stranded threads of miniature stainless steel. This wire is not for wire wrapping! It's meant for stringing beads. The number of wires determines its flexibility: 49 strand is best for bracelets because it is much more flexible than 7-strand. Use crimp beads and tubes with beading wire.

RUBBER TUBING (2)
Available in a variety of colors and diameters, I like to use hollow tubing to cover colored wire, memory wire or flexible beading wire. Cut it up to use it as spacers, or use long lengths to mimic the look of cord.

MEMORY WIRE (3)
Memory wire is tempered wire that "remembers" its shape. It's much too stiff for wire wrapping, but it's perfect for stringing chokers, bracelets and rings. Only use shears that are specially made to cut hardened wire because memory wire will ruin ordinary wire cutters. Finish the ends with a loop, Scrimp finding or end cap.

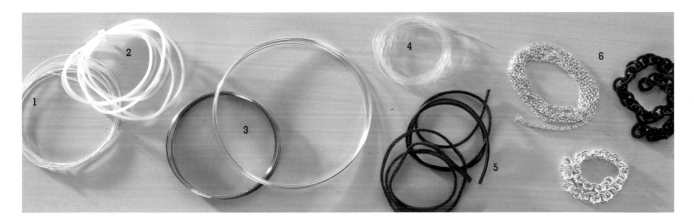

STRETCHY CORD (4, PAGE 7)

Single-strand stretchy cord is available in a variety of colors and diameters. It's great for making fun, stretchy bracelets. Tie the ends in an overhand knot and secure them with jeweler's cement.

LEATHER CORD (5, PAGE 7)

Soft and supple, round leather cord and flat suede lace add textural contrast to wire designs. You could substitute ribbon or another fibrous stringing material for a similar effect.

CHAIN (6, PAGE 7)

Oh, let me count the ways that I love chain. Whether you make your own or use a premade version, chain infuses instant style into your jewelry designs. Layer different styles like patterned links, small cable or polyester chain together for a luxurious look.

....

findings

Mixing metallic findings with colored wire elevates the jewelry and makes it look more stylish. All of the findings in this book are made by Beadalon and are available at your favorite bead shop or craft store.

EZ-CRIMP ENDS (1)

These are my favorite type of ends for flexible beading wire. You place the wire directly into the finding and squeeze the sides to compress the inner coil and hold the wire in place. Some EZ-Crimps already have a clasp attached.

SOLID RINGS (2)

Small solid rings can be used as accents, while large solid rings make great foundations for wire wrapping. The large solid rings in this book are Quick Links by Beadalon.

RING CONNECTORS (3)

These special findings look like miniature staples. Each side can accommodate one Quick Links ring. Use chain-nose pliers to pry each side open to attach it to a ring, then close them to connect two rings together.

CLASPS (4)

Sometimes it's just more convenient to use a premade clasp. I keep a variety on hand, but I particularly like toggles and duet clasps. When you're using a toggle, be sure that the beads near the toggle bar are small enough to pass through the toggle ring.

Learn how to make your own hook clasp on page 120.

KATIEDIDS CREATIVE COMPONENTS (5)

I designed these components to give beaders the power to customize their jewelry, right down to the findings. They're manufactured by Beadalon and are available in a variety of shapes. String beads inside the components for a channel set look.

CRIMP BEADS AND TUBES (6)

These are special metal beads that flatten when squeezed. Choose the size based on the diameter of the beading wire and how many times the wire will pass through the crimp. Use them to attach clasps to the end of flexible beading wire or to hold beaded stations in place on beading wire.

CRIMP COVERS (7)

Cover your crimps with these C-shaped beads for a professional look. They're available in a variety of sizes and finishes. Close them using a Designer Mighty Crimper.

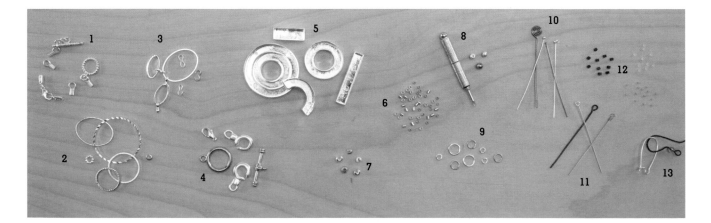

SCRIMP FINDINGS (8, PAGE 8)

Available in different styles for flexible beading wire and memory wire, you can use these findings in place of crimps for beading wire and end caps for memory wire. A tiny set screw holds the wire in place.

JUMP RINGS (9, PAGE 8)

Jump rings provide quick, convenient connections. To close a jump ring, turn the ends past each other until you hear a little *click*, then bring the ends back together for a complete closure. Learn how to make your own jump rings on page 122.

HEAD PINS (10, PAGE 8)

Head pins are thin wires with flattened or decorative ends that prevent beads from sliding off. Use them to make drops and dangles. You can purchase premade head pins or make your own by spiraling a wire end or hammering it into a paddle shape.

EYE PINS (11, PAGE 8)

Eye pins have a single loop, or "eye," on one end that you can use as a connector for jointed dangles. I keep premade eye pins on hand for convenience, but you can turn a basic loop (see page 118) to make your own eye pin from 16-, 18- or 20-gauge wire.

BEAD BUMPERS (12, PAGE 8)

I use these tiny, stretchy beads to hold beads in place on customized ear wires. They come in a variety of colors and shapes. Did I mention they are tiny?

EAR WIRES (13, PAGE 8)

Available in a variety of styles, store-bought ear wires make it easy to make earrings quickly. Learn how to make your own ear wires on page 123.

tools

Good tools make it easier to make jewelry, and you'll have more fun because you'll feel successful. That said, I used "borrowed" tools from my dad's tool bench for a long time before I invested in the proper equipment. When you're ready to build your own toolbox, look for tools with smaller tips that will allow you to work with better precision. Also, give them a test run. Tools should feel good in your hands! You'll be able to work longer and stronger if your hands aren't tired. Good lighting and magnification are also very helpful for successful jewelry making. Wire bits are sharp and they can fly, so it's a good idea to wear safety glasses.

> *In my classes, I encourage my students to stand up and take a break from time to time. We can get so focused on our projects that pretty soon we're all hunched over and tense. This is supposed to be fun! Stretch your arms over your head and lean back a little. Sit on your hands, tuck your chin and bend your neck from side to side. Open your arms wide and draw your shoulders back with your palms open to the front. Breathe!*

CHAIN-NOSE PLIERS (1, PAGE 9)

Chain-nose pliers have tapered, half-round jaws that are smooth inside. Some people use bent chain-nose pliers exclusively, but I switch back and forth between straights and bents, depending on the project. Use the long side of the pliers instead of the tip for more control when opening and closing loops and jump rings.

ROUND-NOSE PLIERS (2, PAGE 9)

Use the tapered, conical jaws of round-nose pliers to make smooth loops. When you're starting out, make loops near the center of the jaws for more control. As your skills increase, you'll be able to make tiny loops at the tip of the pliers.

FLAT-NOSE NYLON JAW PLIERS (3, PAGE 9)

After using chain-nose pliers wrapped with electrical tape for a number of years, I now consider flat-nose nylon jaw pliers essential for wirework. You will also find other styles of nylon jaw pliers, but these are an absolute must-have.

CRIMPING TOOLS (4, PAGE 9)

Crimping tools have special tips that crease, squeeze and round crimp beads and tubes. They come in different sizes that correspond with the sizes of the crimps. A standard crimper is used in most of the beading projects in this book. A Designer Mighty Crimper is great for closing crimp covers.

WIRE CUTTERS (5, PAGE 9)

Some blades are triangular, while others are domed. In either case, choose cutters with sharp, pointy tips. Cushy, ergonomic handles are a plus. For a close cut, always hold the flat part of the blades against the part of the wire that will be left on the work.

MEMORY WIRE CUTTERS (6, PAGE 9)

Learn from my mistakes and don't attempt to cut memory wire with ordinary wire cutters! It will make a notch in the blades. Memory wire cutters have specially hardened blades that can withstand tempered steel.

RING MANDREL (7)

If you're planning to make a lot of rings, it makes sense to add a ring mandrel to your toolbox. The sizes are clearly marked on the mandrel so you can take the guesswork out of sizing. You can place the mandrel inside a vise for extra stability.

HAMMERS (8)

A jeweler's hammer has a wide, smooth side for flattening and a rounded ball peen side for texturing. A nylon hammer prevents marks on the wire surface. Hammering forces the molecules of the metal closer together, which is called "work hardening." You'll need to hammer ear wires, spirals and other flat pieces that you want to retain their shape.

BENCH BLOCK (9)

Use this with a jeweler's hammer to flatten and work harden metal wire. It is heavy and shiny to provide a stable, nonmarring work surface while hammering. Place a leather pad or bench bag underneath to help deaden the sound.

WIRE JIG (10, PAGE 11)

Jigs come in a variety of styles with removable pegs in different sizes that can be placed in the holes to create specific, repeatable patterns. Most jigs are silver or clear. I painted mine white so the wire would show up better.

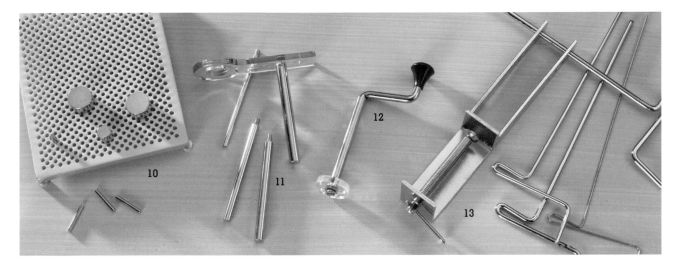

JUMP RING MAKER (11)

Although you can also use the Coiling Gizmo to make jump rings, Beadalon makes several jump ring tools with larger mandrels than the Coiling Gizmo. An acrylic handle makes it a snap to coil wire quickly and easily.

WIRE TWISTER (12)

My favorite twisting tool has an acrylic plate with holes on one end and a crank handle on the other end. If you don't have a wire-twisting tool, you can twist wires together using a power drill or by wrapping the ends around a pencil and turning the pencil.

COILING GIZMO (13)

I'm a fan of the Coiling Gizmo wire-working tool because it's easy to use and it comes with a variety of rods, or *mandrels*, that you can use to make different diameters of coils. Clamp it to your worktable, select a mandrel and you're ready to go. If you don't have a Coiling Gizmo, you can use a chopstick or thin wooden dowel to make the coiled projects in this book.

FILES (14)

You'll occasionally need to file a rough wire end to prevent it from snagging skin or clothing. This is particularly important for the ends of ear wires. There are many different types of files, but my old standby is an emery board that I keep on my desk.

BEADING AWL (15)

You never know when a beading awl will come in handy, so it's best to keep one within reach at all times on your tool bench. I use it to open crimp covers, make holes in bundled wire beads, make precise knots, pry plating out of metal beads, etc. You get the idea.

PERMANENT MARKER (16)

If you accidentally remove a little bit of color from the wire or if a cut end shows copper in a conspicuous place, you can touch it up with a matching permanent marker.

POLISHING CLOTH (NOT SHOWN)

Store jewelry in airtight bags to prevent tarnish. You can use any polishing cloth to clean your wire jewelry.

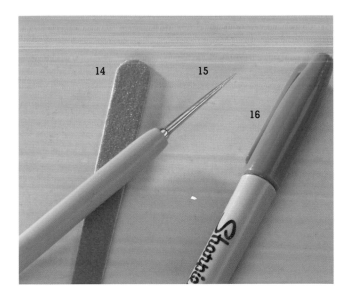

PLAYING WITH *color*

Colored wire + sparkly crystals = a perfect match! Both materials have a lustrous quality that works beautifully together. A color wheel is useful when you're looking for striking combinations, but color inspiration can come from anywhere. Art, nature, fashion magazines and paint chips are just a few great resources. As you flip through the pages of this book, you'll see some of my favorite combinations. Here are a few examples.

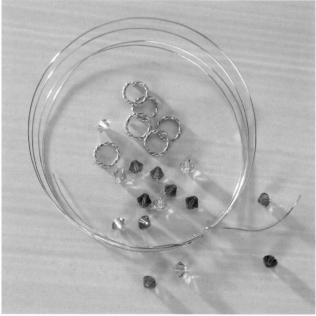

SIAM, LIGHT SIAM, CORAL, RED WIRE

A monochromatic color palette is made of shades of the same color. Monochromatic colors make a cohesive color statement that can be bold or subtle, depending on the color you use. Add depth by including other neutral components such as clear crystals or metallic findings. See the *Siam Bangle Bracelet* on page 28 and the *Lemonade Hoop Earrings* on page 24 for examples.

AQUAMARINE, MONTANA, LIGHT SAPPHIRE, ICE BLUE

Analogous colors are close to each other on the color wheel and create a gentle, pleasing color palette with richer depth than a monochromatic palette. I like these combinations because they're easy to wear with a variety of outfits. The *Favorite Blue Jeans Necklace* on page 18 is a perfect example of a harmonious, analogous color scheme.

PADPARADSCHA, PACIFIC OPAL, INDICOLITE, FILIGREE, COLORED WIRE

Contrasting colors sit directly across from each other on the color wheel, such as orange and blue. I find these combinations a little more challenging, but the results are worth the extra effort. When I acquired the flower for the *Fairy-Tale Filigree Necklace* on page 68, I had to stretch outside my color comfort zone. A favorite ingredient can motivate you to reach a little further!

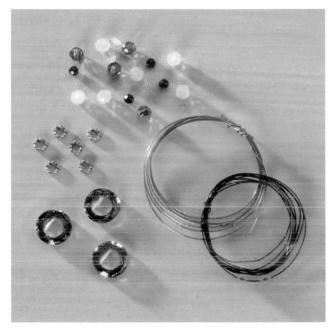

FUCHSIA, GOLD, TOPAZ, BURGUNDY WIRE

My pal and fellow jewelry designer Candie Cooper always says you can't go wrong with a color palette based on a combination you see in nature. I completely agree! One of my favorite flowers is the cosmos. I drew from its natural colors for the *Crystal Volcano Necklace* on page 82.

FROST TUBING, AQUA WIRE, MINT ALABASTER

You can also use colors to replicate the feeling or aspect of something without directly duplicating it. When I was a kid, one of my favorite ice cream flavors was "daiquiri ice" at Baskin-Robbins. You may not see an ice cream cone when you look at the *Crème de Mint Necklace* on page 78, but, to me, this color combination is equally frosty and delicious.

Stuck for color ideas? Check out www.pantone.com for the latest fashion color trend reports. Look for the Pocket Color Wheel at www.colorwheelco.com and the Color Carousel at www.create-your-style.com. Artist Margie Deeb also produces excellent color reports for beaders at www.margiedeeb.com.

····· ⟨∘⟩ ·····

shiny
BRIGHT

Color projects confidence, so build yours with these bright, playful projects. In this chapter, you'll use basic techniques to create playful jewelry that's bright and colorful. Most of the projects use one or two wire-wrapping techniques, from the just-for-fun bundled wire beads on the *Gumball Bracelet* on page 16 to the wrapped wire loops and coils on the *Red Hot Earrings* on page 36. *Lemonade Hoop Earrings* on page 24 are my summery take on this perennial favorite, and the *Siam Bangle Bracelet* on page 28 features one of my favorite tricks for making wide bangle bracelets. You'd better get busy; there are so many ways to shine!

Color inspires your
creative spirit.

gumball
bracelet

This bracelet is just plain fun! Each colorful wire bead is made from about a yard (91.4cm) of wire. You can use leftover pieces of wire or choose the colors specifically to create a particular look. If you're making multiple bracelets, save time by making a bunch of wire beads before assembling the bracelets; they look great stacked together!

MATERIALS

5 crystal 12mm crystal rounds

5 crystal AB lochrose crystal marguerites

24-gauge silver-plated Artistic Wire: rose, plum, fuchsia, tangerine, peacock blue, seafoam green, Christmas green, peach, ice blue, silver blue

0.8mm clear stretchy cord

jeweler's cement

TOOLS

round-nose pliers

chain-nose pliers

wire cutters

beading awl

1. Cut a 1-yard (91.4cm) length of 9 of the wire colors. Cut a 1½-yard (137.2cm) length of the rose wire. Create a total of 10 bundled beads (see *Making a Bundled Wire Bead* on page 118).

2. Working from the spool of elastic cord, string alternating wire beads, crystal marguerites, wire beads and crystal rounds onto the stretchy cord.

3. To tie the cord ends in an overhand knot, make a loop around your fingers. Pass the ends through the loop, then pull them tight.

4. To get the knot closer to the bead, place the tip of the beading awl into the hole of the knot and work the knot closer to the bead.

5. Tighten the knot and add a drop of glue. Let it dry.

6. Cut off the extra cord, then tuck the knot inside the nearest wire bead.

variation

Make quick matching earrings! Make 2 fuchsia bundled wire beads. Cut a 4" (10.2cm) piece of 24-gauge silver wire and center it through a hole on a crystal wild heart pendant. Bend the ends upward and bend each in a right angle above the pendant. Hold the ends together, pass them through a wire bead and make a wrapped loop to attach it to an ear wire. Repeat the assembly to make a matching earring.

FAVORITE
blue jeans
necklace

Y necklaces are the jewelry equivalent of a pair of favorite blue jeans: they're versatile, comfortable and easy to wear. This version features three fancy wire-wrapped links along with a few simpler connections. It's a great example of mixing colored wire with silver findings and chain to create a fashion-forward look. See the variation for instructions to make a quick pair of matching earrings.

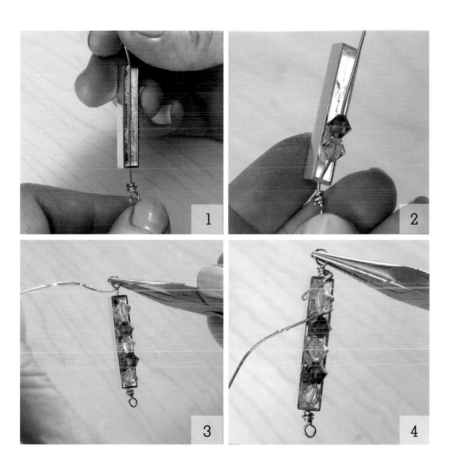

• • • • • ᎶᏋ • • • • •

MATERIALS

10 Montana 6mm crystal bicones

2 indicolite 6mm crystal bicones

1 aquamarine 6mm crystal bicone

2 light sapphire 6mm crystal bicones

1 indicolite 12mm cosmic crystal bead

1 silver 35mm rectangle Katiedids channel finding

22-gauge Artistic Wire: nontarnish silver, ice blue

lengths of silver medium rolo chain: four ¾" (1.9cm), two 4½" (11.4cm)

1 silver medium ball head pin

1 silver EZ-Lobster Clasp

TOOLS

round-nose pliers

chain-nose pliers

wire cutters

1. For the pendant, cut a 14" (35.6cm) length of ice blue wire and make a wrapped loop on one end. Pass the wire through the hole on the channel finding.

2. Pass the wire through the following bicones: light sapphire, Montana, aquamarine, Montana, light sapphire. The beads will sit on top of the channel rather than settling inside.

3. Pass the wire out through the hole on the other end of the rectangle and make a loop.

4. Make a wrapped loop and bring the extra wire downward in a spiral around the edge of the rectangle component and between the bicones.

(steps continue on next page) »

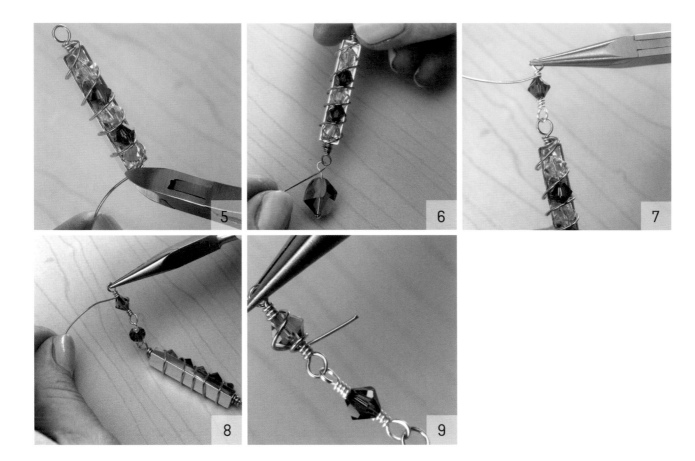

5. Secure the wire end by wrapping it around the base of the opposite loop. Cut off any extra wire.

6. Pass a head pin through a cosmic bead and make a wrapped loop to attach it to the lower loop on the pendant.

7. For the necklace, cut a 3" (7.6cm) length of silver wire and make a wrapped loop to attach it to the upper loop on the pendant. Pass the wire through a Montana bicone and make another wrapped loop (see *Making a Wrapped Link Chain* on page 119).

8. Cut a 4" (10.2cm) length of ice blue wire and make a wrapped loop to attach it to the previous Montana bead link. Pass the wire through an indicolite bicone and make another wrapped loop.

9. Wrap the extra wire around the indicolite bead and around the base of the opposite loop to secure it.

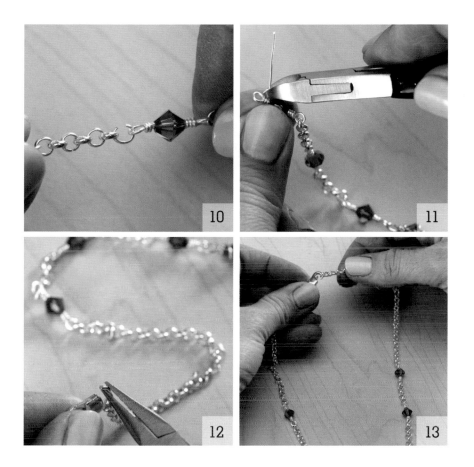

10. Make another Montana bead link, connecting it to the previous indicolite link. Then open the end link on a ¾" (1.9cm) section of chain and attach it to the Montana bead link.

11. Make 2 more Montana bead links, connecting another ¾" (1.9cm) chain between them.

12. Attach a 4½" (11.4cm) chain and the clasp to one end of the necklace.

13. Repeat Steps 7–12 for the other side of the necklace so it's symmetrical. To fasten the necklace, fasten the clasp to the chain on the opposite end.

variation

Cut an 8" (20.3cm) length of ice blue wire and make a wrapped loop to attach it to an ear wire. Slide a 4mm aquamarine bicone and a Bead Bumper onto the ear wire and pinch the ear wire shut above the beaded dangle. Pass the ice blue wire through an indicolite cosmic bead, then make another wrapped loop. Wrap the wire downward in a spiral around the edges of the cosmic bead. Secure it by wrapping tightly around the base of the opposite loop. Make wrapped loops to attach 3 beaded head pins to the lower loop. Repeat to make a matching earring.

CLEVER
coils
bracelet

This quick bracelet looks like a stack of bangles, but it's really one long coil of memory wire that you wrap around your wrist. It also features small wire coils as spacers between the beaded sections. Once you've made the coils, slip them over the memory wire to add texture, color and strength to the design.

MATERIALS

11 crystal copper 8mm crystal rounds

22 Montana 8mm crystal rounds

11 crystal copper 8mm crystal rondelles

24-gauge gun metal Artistic Wire

5 continuous loops of bracelet-size memory wire

66 silver 3.4mm solid rings

2 silver Scrimp finding rounds

TOOLS

wire cutters

memory wire cutters

Coiling Gizmo with thin mandrel*

chain-nose pliers

miniature screwdriver

If you don't have a coiling tool, you can use a piece of 16-gauge wire as a mandrel. Wrap the copper wire around it in a tight coil, then slide it off the wire and cut it into 1" (2.5cm) pieces.

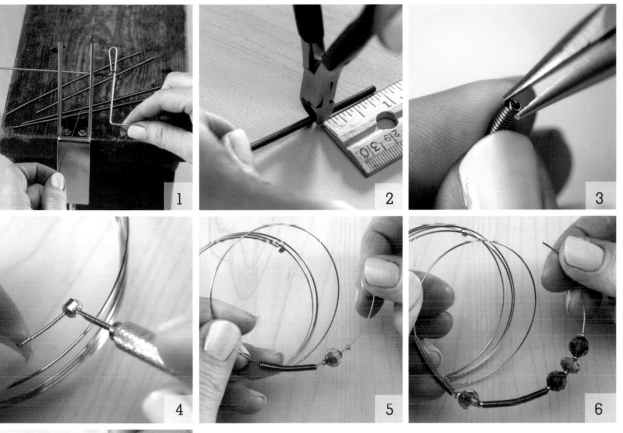

1. Leaving the gun metal wire on the spool, attach the end of the wire to the Coiling Gizmo (see *Using a Coiling Gizmo* on page 121) Turn the handle to create a coil equal to the length of the mandrel. Repeat until you have at least 23" (58.4cm) worth of coils.

2. Cut the wire coils into twenty-three 1" (2.5cm) lengths.

3. Use the chain-nose pliers to press the cut wire ends into the inside of each coil. This prevents snags and allows the beads to sit better on the wire.

4. Use a miniature screwdriver to attach a Scrimp finding to the end of the memory wire (see *Using Scrimp Findings* on page 116).

5. Pass the memory wire through the following: coil, silver ring, crystal copper round, silver ring.

6. Pass the memory wire through the following: coil, silver ring, Montana round, silver ring, crystal copper rondelle, silver ring, Montana round, silver ring.

7. Repeat the beading pattern, alternating units from Steps 5 and 6, until all of the coils and beads are strung. Attach a Scrimp to the end of the memory wire.

LEMONADE HOOP•
earrings

These lemony yellow earrings will surely make any day seem sunnier when you're wearing them! 24-gauge wire is easy to manipulate, but we'll double it to make it strong enough to use for the wrapped cube links. Have fun with these and try making them in your favorite color! The techniques are easy, but the results are impressive, which is just my kind of project.

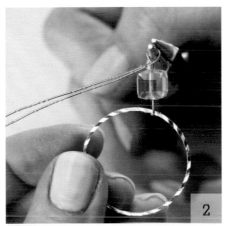

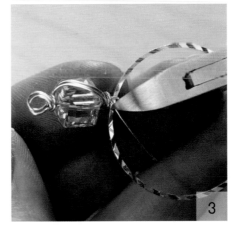

1. Cut a 6" (15.2cm) wire length and fold it in half through one of the silver rings.

2. Hold the wire ends as one and pass them through a cube. Hold the wire ends as one and make a wrapped loop (see *Making a Wrapped Loop Dangle* on page 119).

3. Wrap the wire ends downward around the cube and then coil them several times under the base of the cube. Cut off any extra wire.

(steps continue on next page) »

MATERIALS

34 jonquil 4mm crystal bicones

2 light topaz 8mm crystal cubes

24-gauge lemon Artistic Wire

2 silver 30mm diamond-cut rings

2 silver kidney ear wires

TOOLS

round-nose pliers

chain-nose pliers

flat-nose nylon jaw pliers

wire cutters

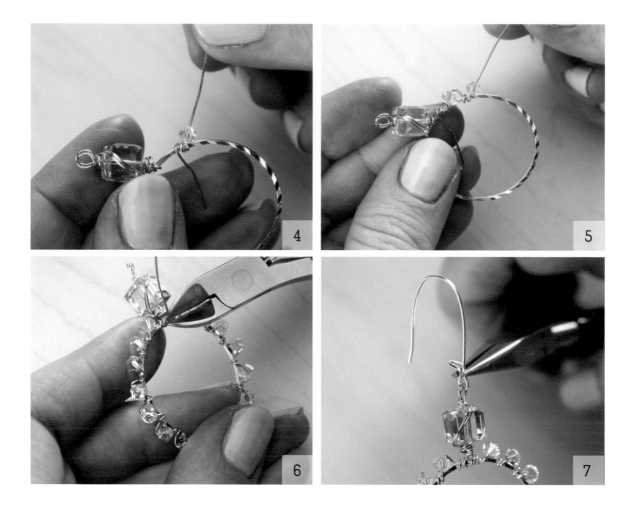

4. Cut a 12" (30.5cm) length of wire and wrap it twice around the silver ring. Pass it through a bicone and wrap one full pass around the edge of the ring.

5. Thread on another bicone and make another complete wrap around the ring.

6. Repeat the technique to wrap 16 total bicones onto the ring. Wrap the wire end twice around the ring and cut off any extra wire. Use the nylon jaw pliers to press the cut ends flush against the ring.

7. Slide the wrapped loop onto an ear wire and pinch the ear wire shut above the dangle.

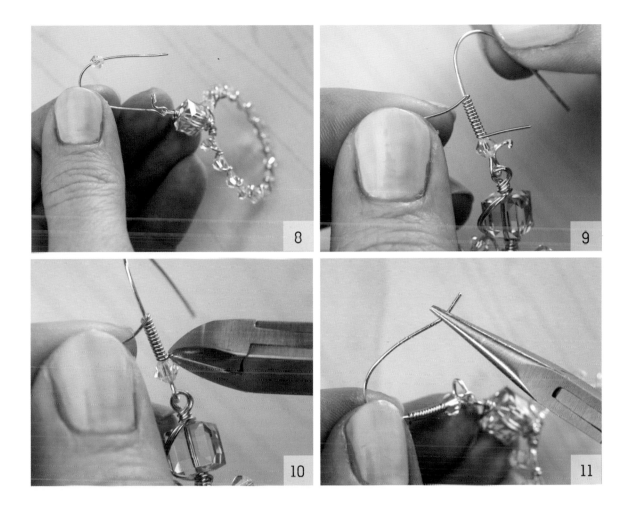

8. Use the chain-nose pliers to straighten the end of the ear wire, then slide a bicone onto the ear wire (see *Embellishing an Ear Wire* on page 123).

9. Cut a 4" (10.2cm) wire length and coil it tightly around the ear wire to hold the bicone in place.

10. Cut the wire ends flush against the ear wire.

11. Bend the ear wire end back to its original slant. Repeat Steps 1–11 to make a matching earring.

SIAM
bangle
bracelet

Even though it isn't the first thing you imagine when you think of memory wire, memory wire actually makes great bangle bracelets. The tempered steel wire provides a good, sturdy structure that you can build up with layers of beads and, in this case, colorful wire coils.

MATERIALS

18 Siam 4mm crystal bicones

64 Siam 6mm crystal helixes*

16 coral 8mm crystal rounds

16 silver sparkle 3mm rounds

32 silver 4mm rondelles

20-gauge red Artistic Wire

22-gauge nontarnish silver Artistic Wire

bracelet memory wire

32 silver eye pins

If you can't find helix-shaped crystal beads but want a similar look, try using graphic cube crystal beads instead.

TOOLS

round-nose pliers

chain-nose pliers

wire cutters

memory wire shears

Coiling Gizmo with thin mandrel*

If you don't have a coiling tool, you can use a piece of 16-gauge wire as a mandrel.

1. Use the Coiling Gizmo and small mandrel to make two 4" (10.2cm) red coils and two 4" (10.2cm) silver coils (see *Using a Coiling Gizmo* on page 121).

2. Cut the red coils into ½" (1.3cm) lengths and the silver coils into ¼" (6mm) lengths. Pass an eye pin through a red coil, sparkle bead and coral crystal; repeat for all of the red coils. Make a basic loop (see *Making a Basic Loop and Bead Link* on page 118). Make sure the loop is facing the same direction as the first loop.

(steps continue on next page) »

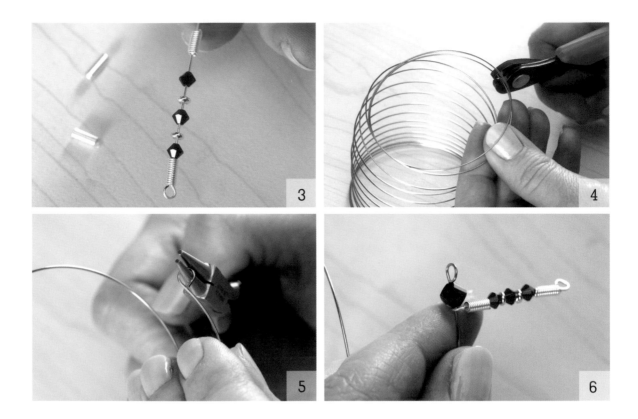

3. Pass an eye pin through the following: silver coil, bicone, rondelle, bicone, rondelle, bicone, silver coil; repeat for all of the silver coils. Make a basic loop. Make sure the loop is facing the same direction as the first loop.

4. Cut 2 loops of bracelet memory wire. To ensure the perfect fit, measure your closed fist across its widest point, then cut 2 memory wire loops that are about 1" (2.5cm) longer.

5. Use the round-nose pliers to make a loop on one end of each memory wire. Unlike ordinary shaping wire, memory wire is actually easier to bend if you turn it against its natural curve.

6. Pass 1 memory wire through a helix bead and a silver coil eye pin loop.

7. Thread the other memory wire through the opposite end of the silver coil eye pin. Make sure the memory wire ends extend in the same direction from the silver coil eye pin.

8. String alternating beads and coiled eye pins, switching the placement of the coral beads as shown. Maintain the bracelet's shape as you string beads; otherwise, the temper of the wire may cause it to spring back and poke you—ouch!

9. After the last bead, make a loop on each wire end. Cut off any extra wire.

10. Hold 2 corresponding end loops together on the bracelet and connect one end of the last red coil eye pin to the loops. Repeat for the other set of end loops.

BERRY
delicious
necklace

Orange crystals add a bright burst to an otherwise analogous color palette of pinks and purples in this colorful necklace. This technique reminds me a little bit of macramé, with the wire wraps taking the place of knots. Use the same technique with an ivory color palette for a gorgeous bridal design.

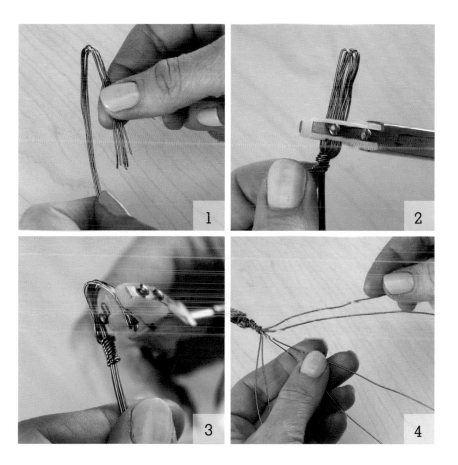

MATERIALS

22 padparadscha 8mm crystal rounds

19 fuchsia 8mm crystal rounds

6 fuchsia 8mm crystal bicones

12 cyclamen opal 8mm crystal rondelles

18 amethyst 10mm crystal bicones

5 amethyst 8mm crystal rounds

5 ruby 15.4mm x 14mm crystal flat briolettes

7½-yard (6.9m) length of 22-gauge amethyst Artistic Wire

35" (90cm) length of 24-gauge purple Artistic Wire

TOOLS

round-nose pliers

chain-nose pliers

flat-nose nylon jaw pliers

wire cutters

1. Cut six 1½-yard (1.4m) lengths of 22-gauge wire. Hold the wires together as one and bend one end back by 1½" (3.8cm).

2. Wrap the wire ends around the base of the fold in a tight coil, then use nylon jaw pliers to press the folded portion together.

3. Bend the folded portion to form a hook (see *Making a Hook* on page 120).

4. Separate the strands into 3 sets of 2 wires each.

(steps continue on next page) »

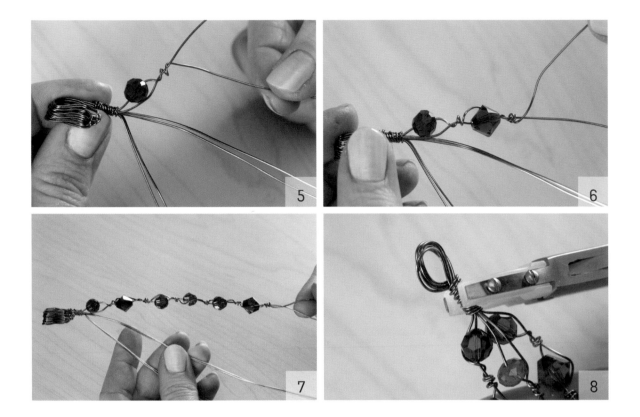

5. Working with one set of wires, pass a wire through an 8mm round bead and wrap this wire around the other wire in the set.

6. Drop the working wire from Step 5 and pass the other wire through an 8mm bicone. Wrap this wire around the dropped wire.

7. Continue the alternating wire-wrap technique to add beads to each set of wires as follows:

   Set 1: Use a pattern of fuchsia round, amethyst bicone, fuchsia round, padparadscha round, repeating until 27 rounds are used.

   Set 2: Use a pattern of cyclamen opal, fuchsia bicone, amethyst bicone, padparadscha round, repeating until 25 rounds are used.

   Set 3: Use a pattern of padparadscha round, amethyst bicone, padparadscha round, amethyst round, fuchsia round, repeating until 25 rounds are used.

8. Hold the wire ends together and bend them into a loop. Wrap the wires around the base of the loop in a tight coil. Use nylon jaw pliers to press the wire ends into the coil.

9. Cut the 24-gauge wire into five 7" (17.8cm) lengths. String a briolette onto the center of the wire and use the chain-nose pliers to bend each wire in a right angle above the briolette's point. Pass the wire ends through a cyclamen opal rondelle.

10. Use the doubled wires to make a wrapped loop, attaching it to the center of the first strand before wrapping it closed (see *Making a Wrapped Loop Dangle* on page 119). Close the loop by wrapping the wire 2–3 times around the wire stem.

11. Wrap the wire downward around the rondelle and 3–4 times around the base of the bead.

12. Repeat Steps 9–11 to attach 4 more briolette dangles evenly spaced on the necklace as shown.

RED HOT •
earrings

This project uses a more traditional coiling method. Instead of making the coil on a mandrel, you wrap the wire directly onto the head pins. Besides adding color and texture to the design, the coiled wire also strengthens the head pins and makes them less likely to bend out of shape above the beaded drops.

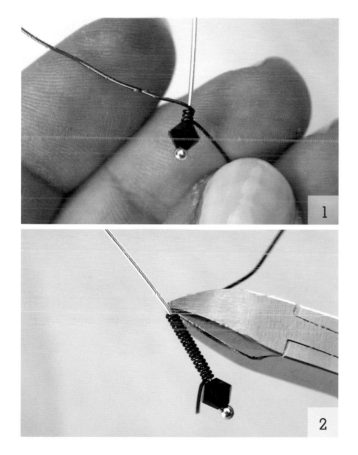

MATERIALS

6 dark Siam 4mm crystal bicones

2 Siam 4mm crystal bicones

2 light Siam 6mm crystal bicones

26-gauge red Artistic Wire

24-gauge silver Artistic Wire

2 silver 4mm solid rings

2 silver diamond 4-loop connectors

6 silver medium ball head pins

2 silver kidney ear wires

TOOLS

round-nose pliers

chain-nose pliers

wire cutters

1. Pass a head pin through a 4mm dark Siam bicone and cut a 4" (10.2cm) length of red wire. Leave a long enough tail that the wire is easy to hold, then wrap it tightly above the bead.

2. Coil the wire for about ⅝" (1.2cm) and then cut off the extra wire at the top of the coil. (It's easier to trim the wire end flush than to try to wrap a short length in such a small, tight coil.)

(steps continue on next page) »

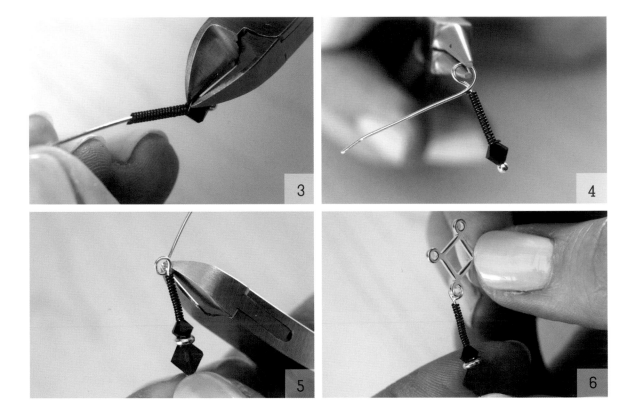

3. Now trim off the wire tail that you were originally holding.

4. Bend the head pin in a basic loop (see *Making a Basic Loop and Bead Link* on page 118). Repeat Steps 1–4 to make a second dangle.

5. Use the same technique to make a coil on a head pin with the following beads: 6mm light Siam bicone, silver ring, 4mm dark Siam bicone.

6. Attach the beaded dangle from Step 5 to the center loop on the 4-loop connector.

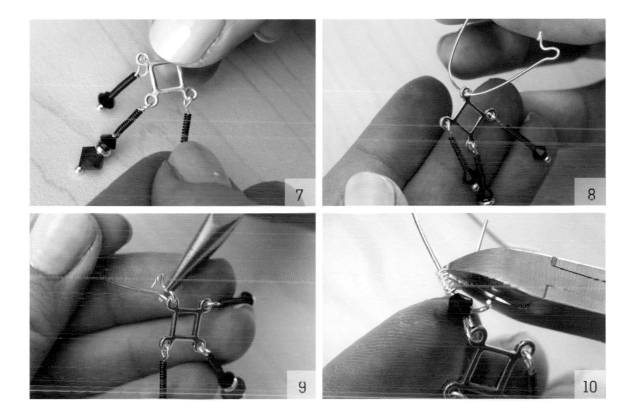

7. Attach the remaining beaded dangles to the outer loops on the 4-loop connector.

8. Thread the upper loop of the 4-loop connector onto an ear wire.

9. Use the chain-nose pliers to pinch the ear wire shut above the dangle.

10. Embellish the ear wire with a 4mm dark Siam bicone (see *Embellishing an Ear Wire* on page 123). Wrap a 2" (5.1cm) length of silver wire in a tight coil above the 4mm bead.

Repeat Steps 1–10 to make a matching earring.

SPARKLETINI *necklace*

The colors of this necklace remind me of fun, fizzy drinks with lots of sparkly bubbles. It features loose, chunky wire wrapping, so you can enjoy the process without worrying about making perfect wraps. The coils in this project are hand-wrapped onto rubber tubing, but you could substitute a thin mandrel with a Coiling Gizmo to achieve a similar effect.

MATERIALS

7 padparadscha 8mm crystal rounds

7 fuchsia 8mm crystal bicones

7 Indian sapphire 8mm crystal rounds

14 silver 3mm sparkle beads

26-gauge plum Artistic Wire

20-gauge peach Artistic Wire

9½" (24.1cm) length of 0.018" (0.5mm) diameter satin silver 19-strand beading wire

6" (15.2cm) length of 1mm frost rubber tubing

silver small cable chain*

silver jump rings: nine 4mm, one 6mm

2 silver no. 1 crimp beads

2 silver 4mm sparkle crimp covers

21 silver ball head pins

1 silver lobster clasp

*The beaded portion of the necklace will measure 8½" (21.6cm); cut 2 equal lengths of chain to fill out the total length of the necklace as desired. I used two 4" (10.2cm) lengths of chain for a 17" (43.2cm) necklace.

TOOLS

chain-nose pliers

wire cutters

crimping tools: standard and Designer Mighty

1

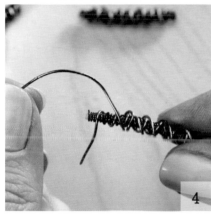

3

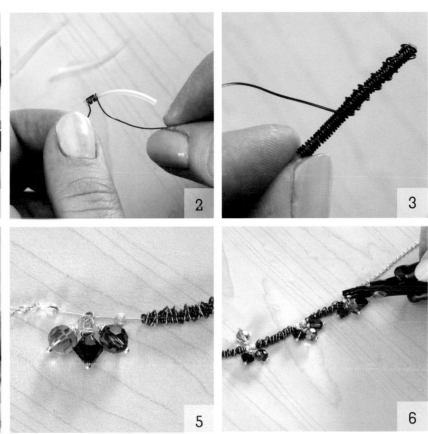

2

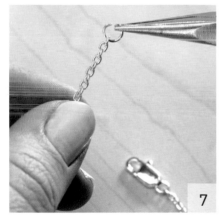

5

6

7

1. Pass a head pin through one 8mm bead and make a loosely coiled wrapped loop (see *Making a Wrapped Loop Dangle* on page 119). Repeat for all of the 8mm beads. Connect one beaded head pin of each color to seven 4mm jump rings.

2. Cut six 1" (2.5cm) lengths of rubber tubing. Working from the spool, coil a piece of plum wire around a piece of rubber tubing from one end to the other. Make sure the coils are close together but not so tight that they close the rubber tubing.

3. Coil the wire again in the opposite direction. Use the chain-nose pliers to press the wire end into the coil.

4. Working from the spool, loosely coil a piece of peach wire in one direction over the plum wire. Coil the peach wire again in the opposite direction. Use chain-nose pliers to press the wire end into the coil. Repeat Steps 2–3 for a total of 6 tube beads.

5. Cut a 9½" (24.1cm) length of beading wire. Pass the beading wire end through a crimp bead, the last link on one piece of chain and back through the crimp bead; crimp it (see *Using Crimp Beads* on page 117). Attach a crimp cover to the crimp bead. Pass the beading wire through the following: jump ring with dangles, sparkle bead, plum/peach coil.

6. Continue the pattern to add alternating sparkle beads, dangles and coils as shown. After the beading pattern is complete, use a crimp bead and cover to attach the beading wire to the remaining length of chain. Trim the excess wire.

7. Use a 4mm jump ring to attach the clasp to one end of the necklace. Connect a 6mm jump ring to the other end of the necklace.

·····ᘒᘙ·····

COOL AS
crystal

Understated elegance is what you'll find with these cool crystal projects that are perfect for everyday wear. Many of the projects in this chapter were inspired by the materials that I used to make them. The sequin-style beads on the *Lochrose Earrings* on page 44 motivated me to make unusual, spiraled connections. For the *Crystal Copper Necklace* on page 48, I made the coils first and then realized that crystal rondelles would make great end caps for the coils. For the *Vintage Garden Necklace* on page 62, I knew I wanted to use the filigree flower as a multiple-strand connector, but it took some experimenting to develop the beaded chain idea.

*Vintage jewelry provides
endless inspiration.*

LOCHROSE • *earrings*

Here's a new way to use spirals to create connections for flat, disk-shaped beads. I chose the marguerite lochrose shape, but you could use this technique with any similar bead that is drilled front-to-back rather than top-to-bottom. This color combination is perfect for everyday wear. Use pearls with crystal AB marguerites for special occasions.

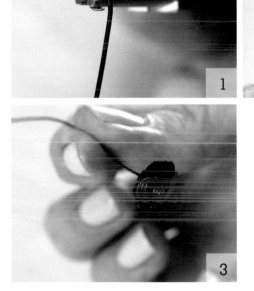

MATERIALS

2 jet 4mm crystal rounds

2 Caribbean blue opal 6mm crystal rounds

2 jet lochrose crystal marguerites

22-gauge Artistic Wire: brown, black

TOOLS

round-nose pliers

chain-nose pliers

flat-nose nylon jaw pliers

wire cutters

nylon hammer and bench block or anvil

wire jig with small and large posts

1. Cut a 6" (15.2cm) length of brown wire and use the round-nose pliers to make a loop on one end of the wire.

2. Hold the loop inside the jaws of the flat-nose pliers and turn your wrist to form a small spiral.

3. Pass the wire through the hole on the marguerite and bend the spiral flat against the front of the bead. Bend the other end of the wire upward against the back of the bead.

(steps continue on next page) »

4. Make a loop above the bead and wrap it twice.

5. Pass the wire end downward across the front of the bead. Wrap the wire behind the spiral. Bring it upward, crossing the bead.

6. Wrap the wire once around the base of the loop.

7. Make sure the wire is securely wrapped around the base of the loop, then cut off any extra wire.

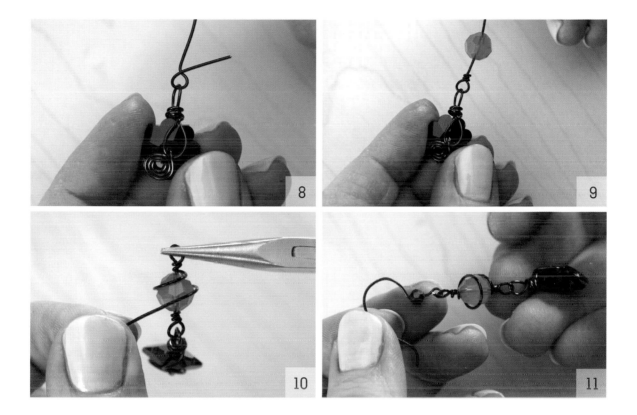

8. Cut a 4" (10.2cm) piece of black wire and make a wrapped loop on one end to attach it to the marguerite dangle (see *Making a Wrapped Link Chain* on page 119).

9. Pass the wire through a 6mm round.

10. Make a wrapped loop and wrap the extra wire downward around the bead. Secure the wire by wrapping it around the base of the original loop.

11. Use 2" (5.1cm) lengths of brown wire and 4mm crystals to make matching ear wires (see *Making an Ear Wire* on page 123). Connect the upper loop of the dangle to the lower loop on an ear wire.

   Repeat Steps 1–11 to make a matching earring.

crystal
copper necklace

Check out the coil links on this matinee-length necklace: they're sandwiched between crystal rondelles. I love this technique for book-ending coils because it's so versatile! You can make links in various lengths and join them together to create all kinds of sleek, colorful designs. Gigantic crystals in alternating colors punctuate this necklace to keep the look fresh and fashion-forward.

MATERIALS

18 crystal golden shadow 8mm crystal rondelles

20 smoked topaz 8mm crystal rounds

3 copper pearl 12mm crystal round

5 crystal copper 18mm large-hole crystal rondelles

5 crystal golden shadow 18mm large-hole crystal rondelles

22-gauge Artistic Wire: copper, brown

TOOLS

Coiling Gizmo with large mandrel*

round-nose pliers

chain-nose pliers

wire cutters

*If you don't have a Coiling Gizmo, substitute a chopstick or thin dowel to create the wire coil.

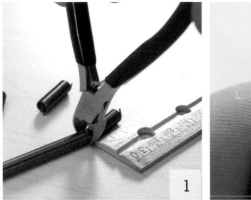

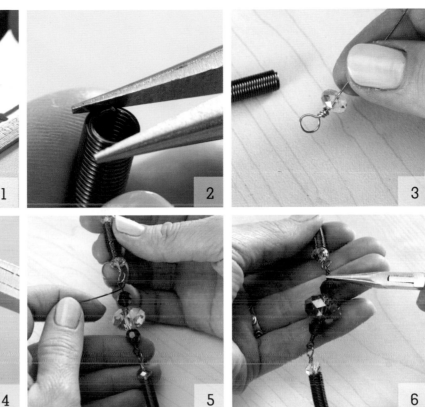

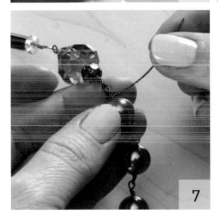

1. Use the large mandrel with the Coiling Gizmo to make two 5½" (14cm) coils using the brown wire (see *Using a Coiling Gizmo* on page 121). Cut the coils into nine ¾" (1.9cm) lengths.

2. Use the chain nose pliers to squeeze the last ring and press the wire end into the center of the coil.

3. Cut a 5" (12.7cm) piece of copper wire and make a large wrapped loop on one end (see *Making a Wrapped Link Chain* on page 119). Pass the copper wire through an 8mm rondelle.

4. Pass the wire through a coil and another 8mm rondelle and make a wrapped loop. Make 8 coil links.

5. Cut a 5" (12.7cm) piece of brown wire and make a wrapped loop to attach it to one of the coiled links. Pass it through a smoked topaz bead, large-hole crystal golden shadow rondelle and another smoked topaz bead. Make a wrapped loop to attach it to another coil link.

6. Cut a 5" (12.7cm) piece of brown wire and make a wrapped loop to attach it to a coiled link. Pass it through a smoked topaz, large-hole crystal copper and another smoked topaz. Make a wrapped loop to attach it to another coil link.

7. Repeat Steps 5–6 until all of the coil links and large-hole bead units are connected. To join the ends of the necklace, use the 12mm pearls with dark brown wire to make connected wrapped loop links.

WINTER
peach
necklace

This necklace started with the pendant, as necklaces often do. The trick with large rings like these is to figure out how to connect them to the rest of the piece. I love the way the bundled wire bead looks really organic and wild sitting atop the square ring! Plus, it provides an excellent way to hide the doubled burgundy wires as they pass upward to create the wire bail.

MATERIALS

14 jet 6mm crystal bicones
1 jet 30mm square crystal ring
22-gauge Artistic Wire:
burgundy, peach, black

TOOLS

round-nose pliers
chain-nose pliers
flat-nose nylon jaw pliers
wire cutters
beading awl
wire twisting tool

1. Use a 2-yard (1.8m) length of wire to make a bundled bead (see *Making a Bundled Wire Bead* on page 118).

2. Cut a 10" (25.4cm) length of burgundy wire and string the jet ring onto the center. Wrap the wire upward around the ring.

3. Cross the wire ends and wrap them around the edge of the ring several times as shown.

4. Use the chain nose pliers to bend the wires at right angles above the top of the ring.

(steps continue on next page) »

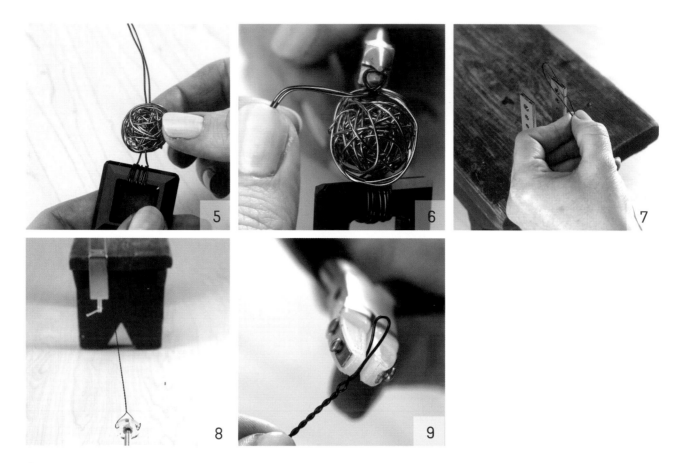

5. Hold the wires together and pass them through the bundled wire bead.

6. Using the burgundy wires as one, make a large wrapped loop (see *Making a Wrapped Loop Dangle* on page 119).

7. Cut a 1-yard (91.4cm) length of black wire and fold it in half. Loop the folded wire over a stable surface (I'm attaching it to the base of my Coiling Gizmo).

8. Use the wire-twisting tool to twist the wires together (see *Making Twisted Wire* on page 121).

9. Use the nylon jaw pliers to press the folded portion of the wire together.

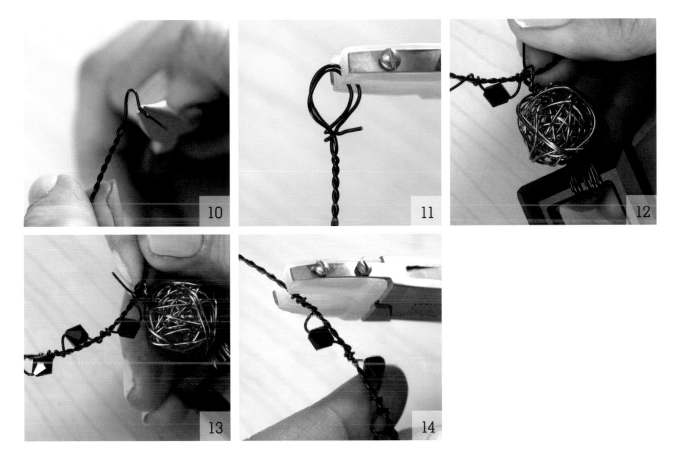

10. Use the chain-nose pliers to bend the folded wire into a hook shape. Turn the end of the hook upward in a short, sharp angle to prevent the clasp from accidentally unfastening.

11. Bend the straightened wire in a large loop, then wrap the wire ends around the base of the loop. (If the wire is very kinked, use nylon jaw pliers to straighten it before making the loop.)

12. String the pendant onto the center of the twisted wires. Cut an 18" (45./cm) length of black wire and coil it twice around the necklace next to the pendant. Add a bicone, then coil it twice again

13. Add another bicone and wrap twice more. Continue for 7 total bicones on this side.

14. Wrap the wire 3 times around the necklace and use the nylon jaw pliers to press the cut end flush against the necklace. Use the same technique to add 7 bicones to the other side of the pendant.

variation

For a quick and easy version, make a similar pendant and slip it onto the center of a simple black cord necklace.

MERLOT HOOP • *earrings*

Hoop earrings make any outfit feel complete, and you can use a little wire wrapping to put your own personal spin on them. Choose hoops in your favorite diameter and adjust the placement of the pegs on the jig as necessary to fill the space across the center of each circle.

MATERIALS

4 vintage rose 4mm crystal bicones

8 burgundy 4mm crystal rounds

2 burgundy 6mm crystal rounds

2 vintage rose 6mm crystal bicones

22-gauge burgundy Artistic Wire

10 silver ball-and-star head pins

6 silver 3.4mm solid rings

2 silver hoop earrings

TOOLS

round-nose pliers

chain-nose pliers

flat-nose nylon jaw pliers

wire cutters

wire jig

nylon hammer and bench block

1. Place your earring on the wire jig. Set one peg toward each outer edge, with three close to each other in the center of the hoop.

2. Cut a 10" (25.4cm) length of wire and wrap it in a tight coil around one side of the hoop.

3. Stretch the wire across the top of the first peg, then wrap it around the peg and over to the next peg.

(steps continue on next page) »

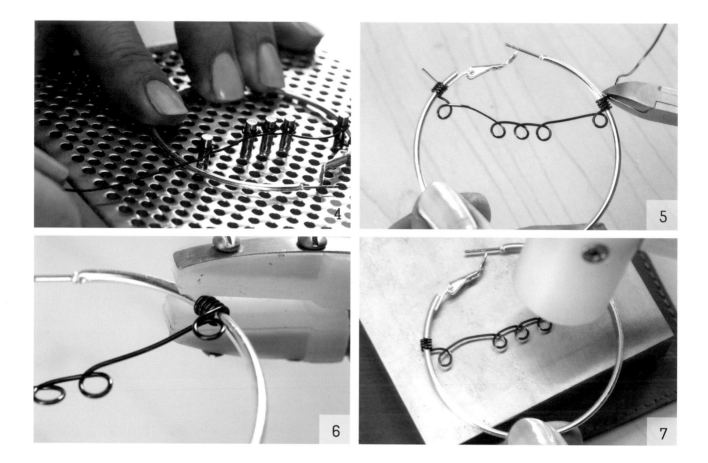

4. Wrap the wire over and then around each peg on the jig.

5. Remove the hoop from the jig. Coil the wire around the edge of the hoop and cut off any extra wire.

6. Use the nylon jaw pliers to press the wire ends flush against the hoop.

7. Use the nylon hammer and bench block to work harden the jigged component.

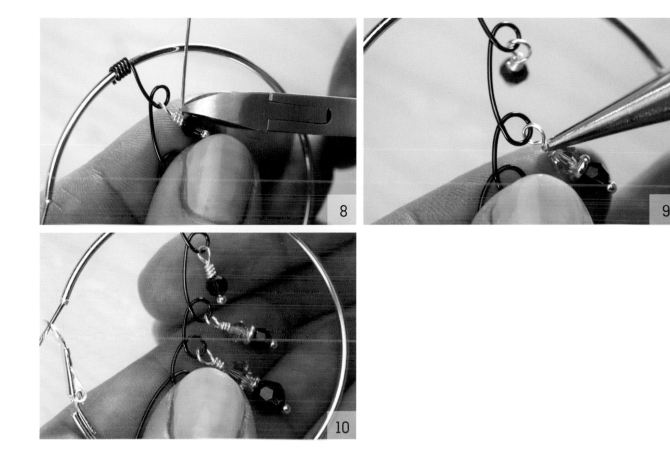

8. Pass a head pin through a 4mm burgundy round and make a wrapped loop to attach it to an outer loop (see *Making a Wrapped Loop Dangle* on page 119). Repeat for the corresponding loop on the other side.

9. Pass a head pin through a 4mm burgundy round, silver ring and a 4mm vintage rose bicone, and make a wrapped loop to attach it to the loop next to the center. Repeat for the corresponding loop on the other side.

10. Pass a head pin through a 6mm burgundy round, silver ring and a 6mm vintage rose bicone, and make a wrapped loop to attach it to the center loop.

Repeat Steps 1–10 to make a matching earring.

jewel candy necklace

I always think crystals look good enough to eat, but alas, they're only beads. This necklace is a grown-up candy necklace for the kid in you. Heavier gauge wire makes it possible to make a connected chain of simple loop bead links, which is the same technique that's often used to make rosaries.

MATERIALS

8 blue zircon 8mm crystal rounds

8 topaz AB 8mm crystal rounds

4 tanzanite 8mm crystal rondelles

13 jet 6mm crystal rounds

3 sunflower 12mm crystal clovers

1 jet 28mm twist crystal pendant

18-gauge nontarnish brass Artistic Wire

14 gold 6mm beaded solid rings

1 gold toggle clasp

TOOLS

round-nose pliers

chain-nose pliers

wire cutters

1. Cut the following lengths of wire: twenty-four 1¼" (3.2cm); four 1¾" (4.5cm) lengths; three 2" (5.1cm) lengths. Use the round-nose pliers to make bead links using the 1¼" (3.2cm) pieces of wire and the 8mm blue zircon and topaz round beads (see *Making a Basic Loop and Bead Link* on page 118), for a total of 16 bead links.

2. Make a large, simple loop on one end of a 1¾" (4.5cm) length and pass it through the following: jet round, gold ring, tanzanite rondelle, gold ring, jet round. Repeat 3 more times for a total of 4 links.

3. Make a large, simple loop on one end of a 2" (5.1cm) length and pass it through the following: jet round, gold ring, clover, gold ring, jet round. Repeat once more for a total of 2 links.

4. Make a large, simple loop on one end of a 2" (5.1cm) length and attach it to the pendant hole.

5. Pass the wire through a gold ring, clover, gold ring and jet round. Make another simple loop, turning the wire to the side so the hole of the loop is visible from the front.

6. Open one loop on a blue zircon link and connect it to the loop above the pendant.

7. Connect a tanzanite link to the blue zircon link.

8. Connect a topaz link to the tanzanite link.

9. Connect bead links in the pattern shown in the image on page 58. Open the last link on each end of the necklace and attach half of the clasp.

TWISTED COIL *bracelet*

Twist three colors of wire together before coiling them to create a tapestry effect. Twisted coils are more substantial than regular coils, so they're less pliable. I used them in short sections in this bracelet because longer sections would prevent the bracelet from curving nicely around the wrist. A woven-looking box clasp perfectly complements the design and makes a pretty focal point, too.

MATERIALS

9 crystal golden shadow 6mm crystal rondelles

9 bronze 8mm × 9mm curved crystal pearls

24-gauge Artistic Wire: gold, gun metal, black

0.018" (0.5mm) diameter gold 49-strand beading wire

18 gold 3.4mm solid rings

18 gold 3mm sparkle rounds

1 round weave 3-strand box clasp

6 gold no. 1 crimp beads

6 gold 3mm crimp covers

TOOLS

crimping tool

wire cutters

Coiling Gizmo with thin mandrel*

wire-twisting tool

3 mini Bead Stoppers (or use adhesive tape, stopper bead, etc.)

*If you don't have a coiling tool, you can use a piece of 16-gauge wire as a mandrel. Wrap the twisted wire around it in a tight coil.

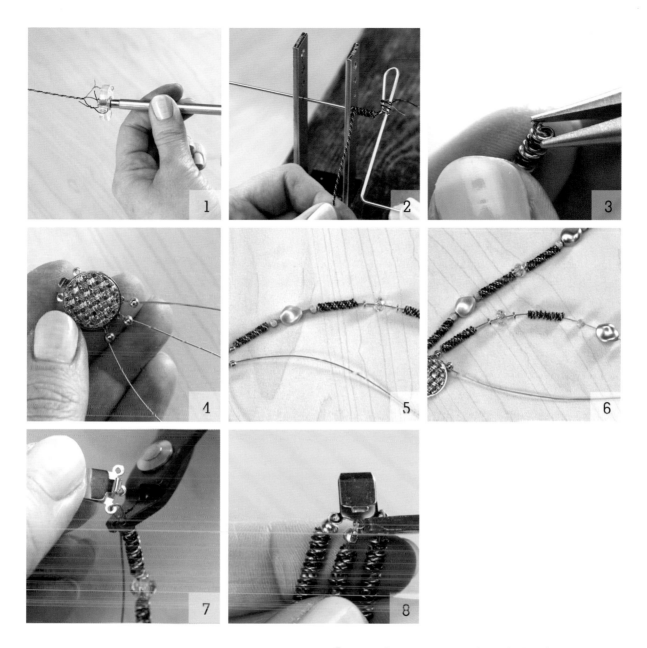

1. Cut three 60" (152.4cm) lengths of each wire: gold, gun metal, black. Attach the wires to the wire-twisting tool and twist them together until one of the end wires breaks—that lets you know that the wire is work hardened and totally twisted (see *Making Twisted Wire* on page 121.)

2. Attach the twisted wire to the Coiling Gizmo and turn the handle to coil the wire (see *Using a Coiling Gizmo* on page 121.)

3. Remove the coiled wire from the mandrel and cut it into 1" (2.5cm) lengths. Use the chain-nose pliers to press the cut ends into the coils to prevent scratching and snagging. Repeat Steps 1–3 to make twenty-one 1" (2.5cm) coils.

4. Cut three 9" (22.9cm) lengths of beading wire. Use a crimp bead and crimp cover to attach each wire to the clasp (see *Using Crimp Beads* on page 117).

5. Pass the upper wire through the following: coil, sparkle, pearl, sparkle, coil, ring, rondelle, ring, coil. Repeat the pattern 2 more times and attach a stopper to prevent the beads from sliding off while you work on the other strands.

6. Pass the center wire through the following: coil, ring, rondelle, ring, coil, sparkle, pearl, sparkle. Add a coil, then repeat 2 more times. Pass through a coil and attach a stopper. For the lower wire, repeat the pattern from Step 5.

7. Check all of the strands to make sure they're even. If they need to be adjusted, you can trim the last coils. Pass the last wire through a crimp bead and attach it to the corresponding loop on the clasp. Crimp it.

8. Attach the 2 remaining wires to the corresponding loops on the clasp. Trim off any extra wire, then add crimp covers to each crimp bead.

VINTAGE
garden
necklace

Asymmetrical necklaces like this one require a lot of planning, but I love making them! It's helpful to place the necklace on a bust while you're linking components together so you can see how the strands drape next to each other. Oxidized chain adds some interest to the design; you can make your own, or use store-bought chain if you're in a hurry.

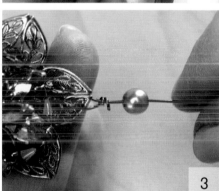

1

2

3

MATERIALS

2" (5.1cm) brass filigree with smoked topaz crystals

2 crystal golden shadow 6mm crystal rounds

6 olivine 6mm crystal bicones

7 bronze pearl 6mm crystal rounds

2 crystal copper 6mm crystal rondelles

8 olivine 8mm crystal bicones

5 smoked topaz 8mm crystal rounds

3 crystal copper 8mm crystal rondelles

6 olivine 12mm × 8mm crystal polygons

1 smoked topaz 18mm × 12mm crystal polygon

22-gauge gun metal Artistic Wire

antique brass unsoldered cable chain

1 gold 16mm twisted solid ring

1 gold box clasp

TOOLS

round-nose pliers

chain-nose pliers

wire cutters

1. Cut a 5" (12.7cm) length of wire and tuck one end into the center of the filigree component between the bezels and the filigree. If necessary, you can add a drop of E6000 or a similar industrial-strength glue to secure it.

2. String six 6mm olivine bicones on the wire and arrange them so they are tucked between the stones on the filigree. To fasten the end, tuck it under the center flower.

3. For the top strand, cut three 3-link sections of chain. Cut a 4" (10.2cm) piece of wire and pass it through a petal on the filigree. Make a wrapped loop, pass the wire through a pearl and make another wrapped loop (see *Making a Wrapped Link Chain* on page 119).

(steps continue on next page) »

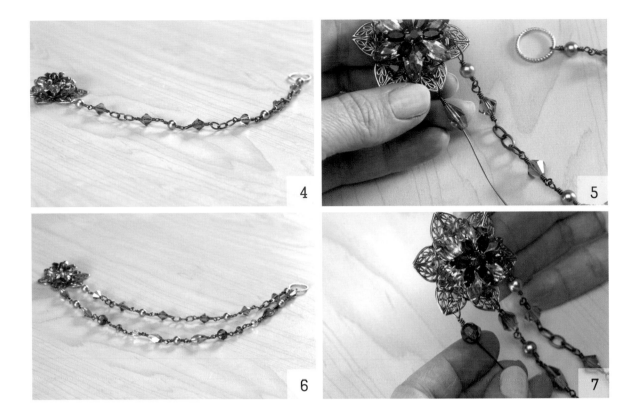

4. Use 4" (10.2cm) lengths of wire to create all beaded links. Link beads and components in the following pattern to create the top chain: 8mm olivine bicone (attached to the pearl from Step 3), 3-link chain, 8mm olivine bicone, pearl, 8mm olivine bicone, 3-link chain, 8mm olivine bicone, pearl, 8mm olivine bicone, 3-link chain, 8mm olivine bicone, pearl. Fasten the last pearl link to the gold twisted ring.

5. Use a 4" (10.2cm) length of wire to make a wrapped loop to attach an olivine polygon to the filigree to start the second strand.

6. Use 4" (10.2cm) wires to create the olivine polygon links and 3" (7.6cm) wires for the other links. Link beads together in the following pattern to create the second chain: pearl (attached to the olivine polygon from Step 5), olivine polygon, smoked topaz round, 6mm crystal copper, golden shadow, olivine polygon, pearl, olivine polygon, smoked topaz round, 6mm crystal copper, golden shadow, olivine polygon, pearl, olivine polygon. Attach the last olivine polygon to the gold twisted ring.

7. Use a 4" (10.2cm) length of wire to make a wrapped loop to attach a smoked topaz round to the filigree, connecting the other end to a 5-link chain.

8. Use 4" (10.2cm) lengths of wire to create all beaded links. Link beads and components in the following pattern to create the bottom chain: 8mm crystal copper (attached to 5-link chain from Step 7), 8mm olivine bicone, 5 link chain, smoked topaz round, 5-link chain, 8mm crystal copper, 5-link chain, 8mm olivine bicone, 5-link chain, smoked topaz round, 5 link chain. Attach the last 5 link chain to the gold twisted ring.

9. Attach an 8mm crystal copper link to the upper petal on the filigree and to a 4½" (11.4cm) piece of chain.

10. Attach the smoked topaz polygon to the gold twisted ring and to a 3½" (8.9cm) piece of chain.

11. Attach half of the clasp to each end of the necklace.

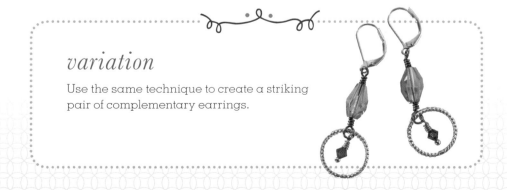

variation

Use the same technique to create a striking pair of complementary earrings.

·····❦·····

sparkly & SWEET

You can't beat crystals for sparkle, and these sweet projects won't disappoint. From the *Rosy Outlook Earrings* on page 72 to the *Crystal Volcano Necklace* on page 82, you'll combine several wirework techniques to create fashionable jewelry. Look to the *Springtime Choker* on page 74 for a primer on making beaded flowers, which is one of my favorite wirework techniques. The *Fairy-Tale Filigree Necklace* on page 68 is a vintage-inspired design with a modern twist, and the *Crème de Mint Necklace* on page 78 is a lesson in creating graduated strands. The *Very Violet Necklace* on page 86 is one of my most popular workshops and features my very own Katiedids Creative Components. Enjoy!

Crystals are a beader's best friend.

FAIRY-TALE *filigree* necklace

The unexpected color combination in the filigree flower inspired the design for this necklace. I wanted to combine the flower with wirework and chain, so I chose the open circle chain because it would be easy to customize with nestled beads inside the links. Wear it asymmetrically with the flower section on one side and you'll look straight out of a fairy tale.

· · · · · 🎵 · · · · ·

MATERIALS

4 padparadscha 4mm bicones

8 indicolite 5mm bicones

13 Pacific opal 6mm cubes

4 padparadscha 8mm rounds

4 indicolite 8mm rounds

25mm filigree flower with padparadscha and Pacific opal stones

20-gauge and 24-gauge nontarnish brass Artistic Wire

12 gold medium ball head pins

gold Quick Links chain with 31 connected 14mm rings

TOOLS

round-nose pliers

chain-nose pliers

wire cutters

flat-nose nylon jaw pliers

1. Cut six 3" (7.6cm) lengths of 20-gauge wire. Make a wrapped loop to attach one 3" (7.6cm) wire to the flower (see *Making a Wrapped Loop Dangle* on page 119). Pass the wire through a cube and complete the wrapped loop.

2. Use a 3" (7.6cm) wire length to make another cube link attached to the first. To do this, turn the loop on the new piece of wire and thread it through the closed loop on the end of the finished link. After threading, proceed with wrapping the loop (see *Making a Wrapped Link Chain* on page 119).

(steps continue on next page) »

3. Make another cube link, attaching the last loop to a ring on the chain.

4. Repeat Steps 1–3 to connect 3 cube links and the other end of the chain to the other end of the flower.

5. Pass a head pin through an indicolite bicone and make a wrapped loop to attach it to the connector between 2 cubes.

6. Repeat Step 5 to attach another matching head pin to the same link. Repeat Steps 5–6 to attach 2 indicolite bicones between each set of cubes as shown. Make wrapped loops to attach a padparadscha bicone head pin to the other loop between each set of cubes.

tip

Like a nametag, the focal components of an asymmetrical necklace should always be worn on your right side.

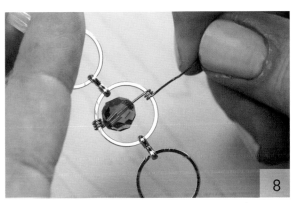

7. Cut fifteen 2½" (6.4cm) lengths of 24-gauge wire. Wrap the end of a piece of wire 3 times over the edge of the second ring on the chain. Pass the wire through a padparadscha round, then under the opposite edge of the ring.

8. Wrap the wire 3 times around the edge of the circle, with the wire coiling toward the opposite end of the circle as the wrapped wire in Step 7.

9. Trim the wire ends so the cut end lays against the inside edge of the ring.

Repeat the nestled-bead technique for every other ring on the chain, alternating 8mm crystals as follows: padparadscha round, Pacific opal cube, indicolite round, Pacific opal cube.

variation

Make a quick pair of earrings to match! Use 24-gauge wire to nestle 8mm padparadscha rounds inside 14mm rings. Make wire-wrapped links to attach 6mm cubes to kidney ear wires. Embellish the ear wires with 4mm indicolite bicones held in place by Bead Bumpers.

ROSY OUTLOOK •
earrings

Although chandelier earrings are standard for dressy occasions, they also raise the wow factor for everyday outfits. Make them in your favorite color and I'm sure these will become your go-to pair! Handmade wire components mean they're uniquely yours, while silver chain and earring findings make it easy to whip them up.

MATERIALS

2 light rose 4mm rounds
2 rose 6mm × 9mm teardrops
20-gauge rose Artistic Wire
2 silver ball-and-star head pins
4 silver 4mm jump rings
small silver cable chain
2 silver kidney ear wires
2 clear oval Bead Bumpers

TOOLS

wire jig
hammer and bench block
round-nose pliers
chain-nose pliers
wire cutters

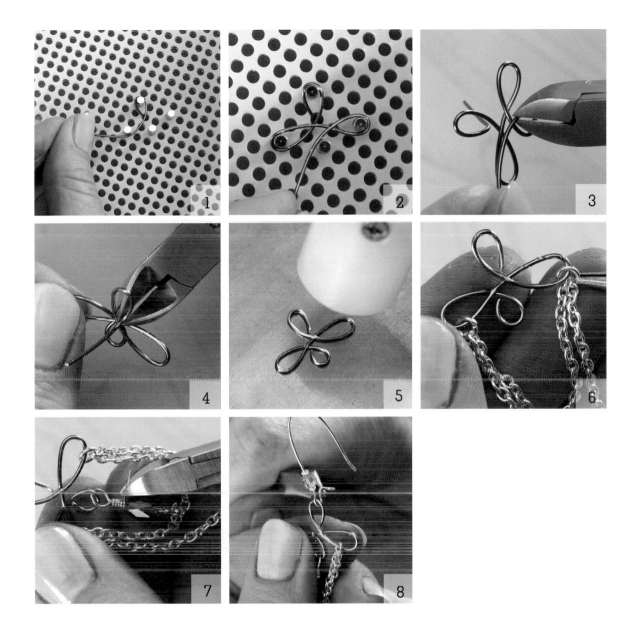

1. Set 4 pegs in the pattern shown on the wire jig. (Note: For demonstration purposes, I painted my jig white with spray paint.) Cut a 4½" (11.4cm) length of rose wire and place one end into a hole near the first peg.

2. Wrap the wire around the pegs in a cloverleaf pattern.

3. Remove the cloverleaf from the wire jig and trim the excess wire from one loop.

4. Trim the excess wire from the other end of the cloverleaf.

5. Place the wire design on the bench block and strike it with a hammer to work harden the wire.

6. Cut the following lengths of chain: one 2¾" (7cm) and one 2¼" (5.7cm). Hold the lengths together and use a jump ring to connect the ends to a large loop. Use a jump ring to connect the opposite ends of the chain to the large loop on the opposite side of the wire component.

7. String a teardrop onto a head pin and make a wrapped loop to attach it to the small loop on the wire component (see *Making a Wrapped Loop Dangle* on page 119).

8. String a Bead Bumper, a 4mm round and a Bead Bumper onto a kidney ear wire. String the wire component onto the ear wire and then use the chain-nose pliers to squeeze the ear wire together to hold the wire component in place.

Repeat Steps 1–8 to make a matching earring.

springtime choker

I get a lot of questions from my blog readers about making bead and wire flowers. This is one of my favorite techniques; you just string a bead onto a wire, bring the wire downward to the base of the bead and twist the wires together to form a petal. The leaves use the same technique, but you twist the wires together a little more to form stems or branches.

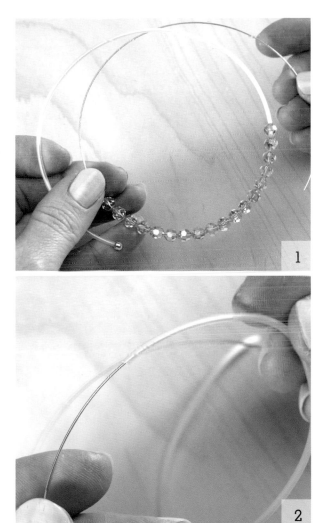

MATERIALS

6 crystal AB 4mm rounds

3 vintage rose 6mm bicones

18 light rose AB 6mm rounds

10 rose 9mm x 6mm teardrops

4 crystal AB 12mm bicones

24-gauge nontarnish silver Artistic Wire

1½ loops of continuous necklace memory wire

1mm frost rubber tubing

2 silver memory wire Scrimp findings

TOOLS

miniature screwdriver

round-nose pliers

chain-nose pliers

wire cutters

flat-nose nylon jaw pliers

memory wire cutters

1. Use a miniature screwdriver to attach a Scrimp finding to one end of the necklace (see *Using Scrimp Findings* on page 116). Pass the wire through a piece of 7¾" (19.7cm) rubber tubing and all the 6mm rounds.

2. Add another piece of 7¾" (19.7cm) rubber tubing. Attach a Scrimp finding to the end of the wire. (It's okay if there is some empty space on the wire.)

(steps continue on next page) »

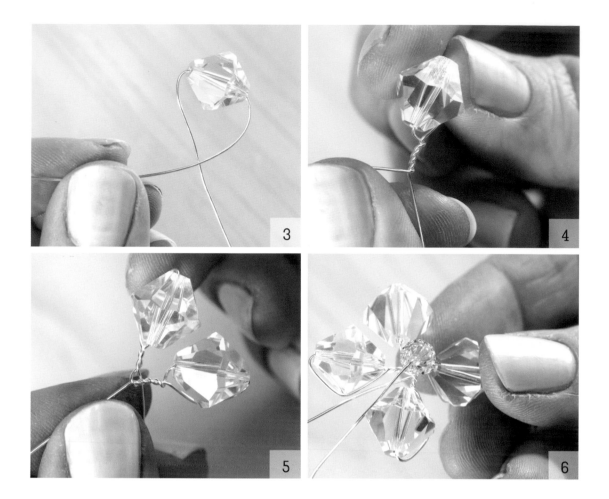

3. For the center flower, cut a 12" (30.5cm) wire length and center it through a 12mm bicone.

4. Bring the wire ends downward against the bead and twist the wires together at the base.

5. Leave about ¼" (6mm) and repeat Steps 3–4 to make another petal. Continue adding beads and twisting together until all of the petals are formed. Work on both sides of the first petal so the wire ends remain about even.

6. Pass the wire through a 6mm bicone and wrap it across the center of the flower.

tip

Don't twist the wire too much or it may snap off—just a few good turns will do!

7. Wrap the wire ends of the center bead in opposite directions around the center beads on the choker to secure the flower placement.

8. Use 12" (30.5cm) wire lengths with 5 teardrops and a 6mm bicone to make 2 pink daisies using the same technique.

Make 2 twisty leaves using this modified flower technique: Use a 6" (15.2cm) length of wire and 3 AB 4mm rounds for each leaf. Slide the first crystal onto the center of the wire and twist the wires together. Leave a ¼" (6mm) space and pass the wire through a second round and twist it. Repeat on the other side of the wire for the third round. Twist the wires together for ½" (1.3cm).

9. Wrap the wire ends in opposite directions around the 6mm rounds to attach the daisies to the necklace on each side of the center flower. Attach a twisty leaf behind each daisy.

10. If you do have space between the rubber tubing and Scrimp ends, wrap a small amount of wire between the beads and the tubing to help push the tubing against the Scrimp.

CRÉME DE
mint
necklace

Graduated necklaces are always in style. This project is a good example of using wire to enhance a simple beaded design. The thin-gauge aqua wire adds color and a handmade element, which takes it to the next level.

MATERIALS

14 mint alabaster 6mm rounds

26 mint alabaster 8mm rounds

16 bronze 6mm pearls

16 bronze 10mm pearls

2¾-yards (2.5m) 26-gauge aqua Artistic Wire cut into twenty-five 4" (10.2cm) pieces

1½-yards (1.4m) 0.018" (0.5mm) diameter silver 19-strand beading wire cut into one 16" (40.6cm) length; one 18" (45.7cm) length; and one 20" (50.8cm) length

27½" (69.9cm) 1mm frost rubber tubing cut into two 1½" (3.8cm) pieces; two 2" (5.1cm) pieces; two ½" (1.3cm) pieces; and twenty-one 1" (2.5cm) pieces

48 silver 6mm beaded solid rings

1 silver 3-loop slide clasp

6 silver-lined crimp covers

6 silver no. 1 crimp beads

TOOLS

standard crimping tool
Designer Mighty Crimper
wire cutters
flat-nose nylon jaw pliers
tape or bead stoppers

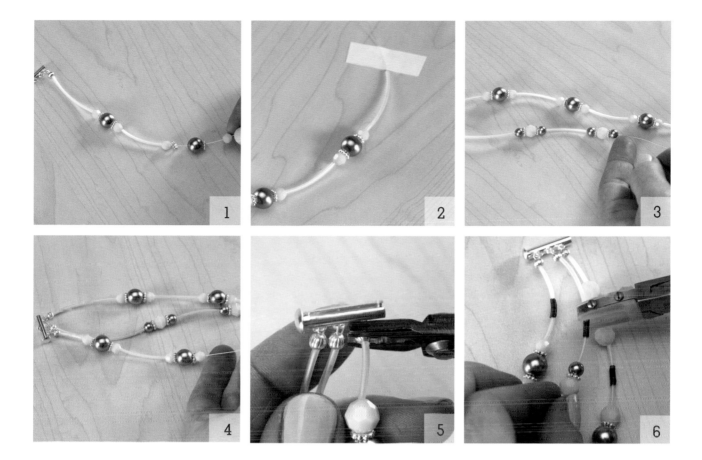

1. Crimp the 16" (40.6cm) wire to the top loop on the clasp (see *Using Crimp Beads* on page 117) and string on a 1½" (3.8cm) piece of rubber tubing. Then string on the following pattern: 6mm mint alabaster, silver beaded ring, 10mm bronze pearl, silver beaded ring, 6mm mint alabaster. Then string on a 1" (2.5cm) piece of rubber tubing. Repeat the bead pattern a total of 7 times, placing a 1" (2.5cm) piece of rubber tubing between each repeat.

2. After stringing on the final bead pattern section, string on a 1½" (3.8cm) piece of rubber tubing and tape the end of the wire to your work surface or add a bead stopper to secure the strand.

3. Crimp the 18" (45.7cm) stringing wire to the middle loop of the clasp and string on a 2" (5.1cm) piece of rubber tubing. Then string on the following bead pattern: 6mm bronze pearl, silver beaded ring, 8mm mint alabaster, silver beaded ring, 6mm bronze pearl. Then string on a 1" (2.5cm) piece of rubber tubing. Repeat the bead pattern a total of 8 times, placing a 1" (2.5cm) piece of rubber tubing between each repeat. After stringing on the final bead pattern section, string on a 2" (5.1cm) piece of rubber tubing and secure the strand.

4. Crimp the 20" (20.8cm) stringing wire to the bottom loop of the clasp and string on a ½" (1.3cm) piece of rubber tubing. Then string on the following pattern: 6mm mint alabaster, silver beaded ring, 10mm bronze pearl, silver beaded ring, 6mm mint alabaster. Then string on a 1" (2.5cm) piece of rubber tubing. Repeat the bead pattern a total of 9 times, placing a 1" (2.5cm) piece of rubber tubing between each repeat. After stringing on the final bead pattern section, string on a ½" (1.3cm) piece of rubber tubing and secure the strand.

5. Adjust the necklace as desired and, one at a time, crimp the strands to the corresponding loop on the opposite end of the clasp.

6. Wrap the lengths of aqua wire around the center of each 1" (2.5cm) rubber tubing length. Trim the excess wire as needed.

For the ends of the 18" (45.7cm) and 20" (50.8cm) strands, wrap the aqua wire around the tubing ⅜" (1cm) from the last bead units.

Use the nylon jaw pliers to press the ends of the coils into the rubber tubing to prevent snags.

COSMO •
ring

Named after a fashionista's favorite cocktail, this sparkly ring is enough to make your mouth water. The secret to capturing the crystals is in the weaving technique you use for creating the beaded section. It's like the perfect outfit: it takes some work to achieve but looks effortless when you're done. The ring would look totally different but equally spectacular in a subtler color palette.

MATERIALS

3 hyacinth 4mm bicones
3 padparadscha 4mm bicones
2 light sapphire 4mm bicones
2 air blue opal 8mm bicones
2 padparadscha 8mm rounds
22 gauge peach Artistic Wire

TOOLS

flat-nose nylon jaw pliers
chain-nose pliers
wire cutters
ring mandrel

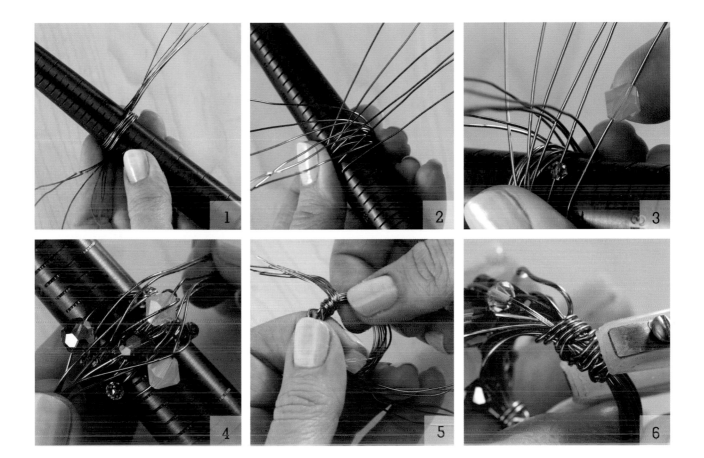

1. Cut six 12" (30.5cm) lengths of wire and bend them loosely in half. Place the fold over the ring mandrel two sizes larger than the desired ring. Wrap the wire ends all the way around the mandrel so they are back in front.

2. Adjust the wires so they alternate one from the left, one from the right, etcetera, until the wire ends are loosely woven together in front of the mandrel.

3. Slide a bead onto each wire, keeping the beads centered over the top of the mandrel. Alternate bead colors and sizes on the wires.

4. Adjust the beads if necessary so they're bundled as shown. Fold the wires loosely to the sides of the mandrel.

5. Remove the ring from the mandrel, holding it tightly to preserve the shape. Coil the wires around one side of the beaded section. Repeat for the other side of the ring.

6. Trim the ends and press them into the coiled band to prevent snagging on skin or clothing. Use the nylon jaw pliers to press the coiled sections to make them tight and secure.

CRYSTAL *volcano* necklace

In this project, you'll make your own custom chain to form the foundation for a show-stopping necklace. Even if you just make the chain, you'll have a wearable piece of jewelry. But, if you're like me, you won't be able to resist adding layers of crystals to create a dramatic statement necklace. Either way, you're in for some fun!

MATERIALS

5 crystal volcano 14mm cosmic rings

11 fuchsia 4mm rounds

11 topaz AB 6mm rounds

11 rosewater opal 6mm rounds

11 Indian sapphire 6mm rounds

22-gauge Artistic Wire: burgundy, nontarnish brass

77 gold 6mm beaded solid rings

28 gold medium ball head pins

1 gold toggle clasp

TOOLS

round-nose pliers

chain-nose pliers

wire cutters

jump ring maker with 8mm mandrel

wire-twisting tool

1. Use the wire-twisting tool to twist 2 strands of burgundy wire together (see *Making Twisted Wire* on page 121). Remove the twisted wire from the tool and use the jump ring maker to make a coil. Use wire cutters to snip the rings off of the coil (see *Making Jump Rings* on page 122). You'll need a total of 21 rings.

2. Use the wire cutters to snip through 22 gold rings so you can use them as connectors.

(steps continue on next page) »

3. Using the chain-nose pliers, slip the closed jaws into the center of a gold ring. Open the pliers and gently force the cut open.

4. Use the cut gold rings to connect 2 uncut gold rings, using the chain-nose pliers to close the rings. Make 22 sets of 3 rings each.

5. Make a chain by alternating the gold ring sections and the twisted rings. You should begin and end with gold ring sections.

6. Make the following dangles (see *Making a Wrapped Loop Dangle* on page 119):

6 fuchsia/beaded ring/topaz dangles on ball head pins.

11 rosewater opal dangles on ball head pins.

5 cosmic ring dangles. To make these, cut a 4" (10.2cm) piece of nontarnish brass wire and make a large loop. Slip the loop onto a cosmic ring and wrap it closed. Using one of the remaining wires, add a fuchsia bead, gold ring and a topaz bead and make a wrapped loop. Trim the excess wire.

11 Indian sapphire dangles on ball head pins.

7. Starting from one end of the chain, count to the sixth twisted ring. On the sixth ring, thread on the following dangles: Indian sapphire, fuchsia/beaded ring/topaz, rosewater opal.

8. On the next ring (the seventh), thread on the following: rosewater opal, cosmic ring, Indian sapphire.

9. Repeat Steps 7–8 until all the dangles are used. Attach the toggle clasp components on the ends of the chain.

variation

Use the same technique to make matching earrings. Embellish the ear wires with gold sparkle beads held in place by Bead Bumpers.

VERY •
violet
necklace

This is one of my best-selling workshops. I've taught it at the Bead and Button Show and the Create Your Style in Tucson event. The loose basket weave technique is a great way to embellish any kind of large link or geometric chain.

MATERIALS

3 Katiedids Creative Components 5-hole round donut

assorted 4mm–6mm amethyst and violet opal beads

12 violet opal 4mm rounds

6 amethyst 6mm rondelles

4 silver Quick Links ovals

silver round link chain

24-gauge purple Artistic Wire 0.015" (0.4mm) diameter

19-strand beading wire

6 silver head pins

1 silver duel clasp

TOOLS

chain-nose pliers

wire cutters

flat-nose nylon jaw pliers (optional)

1. Cut a 16" (40.6cm) length of purple wire. Wrap one end of the wire 3 to 4 times around the oval's edge as shown. Pass the wire through a bead, then wrap it around the opposite side of the oval.

2. Weave your way back and forth across the oval, adding beads as you work from one end to the other. When you reach the opposite end of the oval, wrap the wire tail 3 to 4 times around the oval's edge and trim the excess wire. Repeat Steps 1–2 for a total of 4 ovals.

(steps continue on next page) »

3. For each donut, pass a head pin through a hole from the center extending outward. String a 6mm amethyst rondelle onto the head pin, then make a wrapped loop to connect it to a wire-wrapped oval.

4. Repeat for the other end of the donut so the focal section pattern is: oval, donut, oval, donut, oval, donut, oval.

5. Cut a 5" (12.7cm) length of the beading wire. In one of the donuts, pass the beading wire under the exposed head pin shaft. String 2 violet opal 4mm rounds onto one side of the beading wire. To the other side, string on 7 violet opal 4mm rounds

6. Using the beading wire that has the 7 beads, thread the tail under the remaining exposed head pin shaft.

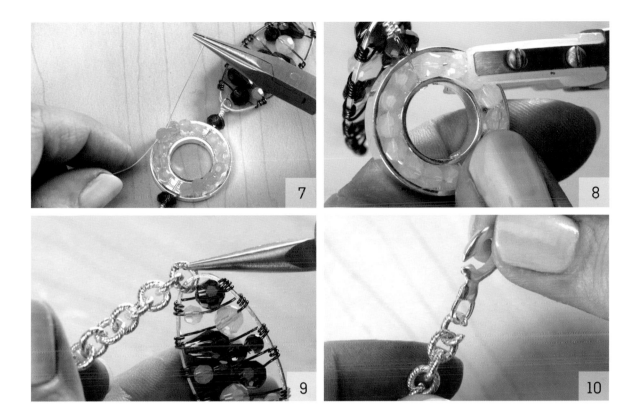

7. To the 2-bead strand, add 2 more beads. Add 3 beads to the other stringing wire tail. Pass the end of the 3-bead tail into the fourth bead of the opposite tail and pull tight.

8. Gently press the beaded loop into the channel of the donut component. The nylon jaw pliers are especially useful. You can add a drop of jeweler's cement for extra security.

9. The beaded portion of the necklace measures approximately 11¼" (28.6cm); cut the round link chain into 2 equal lengths that will give you the desired total length. I used two 2½" (6.4cm) lengths of chain for a 17" (43.2cm) necklace. Open the last link on each chain and attach one to each side of the necklace focal section.

10. Open the last link on the opposite end of each side of the necklace and attach half of the clasp.

variation

Use the same technique to embellish a circle link. Attach it to a chain for a quick pendant.

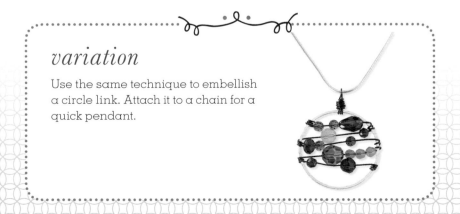

·····ᘓᘗ·····

one
OF A KIND

Take a creative journey through this collection of projects featuring a variety of wirework techniques from wrapping to twisting, weaving and more. These luxe, layered designs are easy to alter to reflect your own unique style. Mix it up with twisted wire, rings and oodles of dangles on the *Bronze Baubles Necklace* on page 94 or keep it cool and collected with the artsy *Jet-Setter Bangles* on page 106. The *Street Smart Necklace* on page 102 is based on a necklace I made and have worn to conventions for years as a badge lanyard because it goes with every outfit. Make eye-catching *Emerald Chain Maille Earrings* on page 98, or try your hand at a truly unique piece, the *Twisted Treasure Necklace* on page 112.

Make a statement with
jewelry as unique as you.

mermaid's
rings necklace

I'm addicted to this wire-weaving technique for embellishing store-bought chain! There are so many possibilities. You could combine just about any collection of 4mm–6mm beads to put your own unique stamp on your favorite chain. Use 24-gauge wire because it's easy to manipulate but holds its shape on these small frames. This asymmetrical necklace works up quickly and is sure to garner lots of compliments.

MATERIALS

For the links: assorted 4mm–6mm Capri blue and Caribbean blue opal rounds, bicones and rondelles (as shown: 13 Capri blue 4mm bicones, 6 Capri blue 6mm bicones, 6 Caribbean blue opal 6mm rondelles, 6 Caribbean blue opal rounds)

For the dangles: 10 Caribbean blue opal rounds, 10 Capri blue bicones

24-gauge silver blue Artistic Wire

20 silver medium ball head pins

silver Quick Links chain with alternating small/large ovals

TOOLS

round-nose pliers

chain-nose pliers

wire cutters

flat-nose nylon jaw pliers

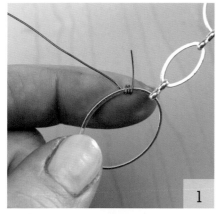

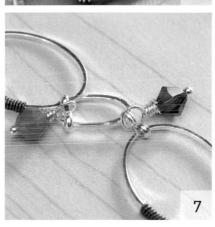

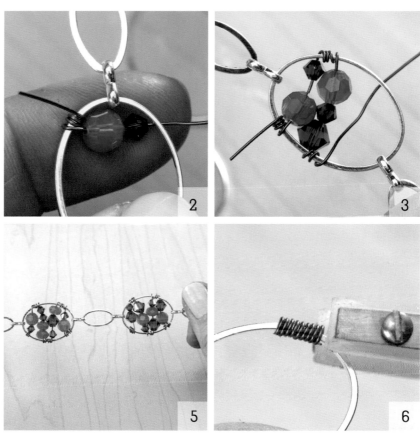

1. Cut three 10" (25.4cm) lengths of 24-gauge wire. If your chain is not connected into one continuous loop, connect the ends. Wrap one end of the wire 3 times over the edge of a large oval link with the wrapped wire extending toward the closest end of the oval.

2. Pass the wire through 2 to 3 random beads and under the opposite edge of the oval link.

3. Wrap the wire 3 times around the edge of the link with the wrapped wire extending toward the farthest end of the oval.

4. Pass the wire through 2 to 3 more beads, weave it under the opposite edge of the oval link and wrap it around.

5. Repeat Steps 1–2 for 2 more large oval links on the chain.

6. Cut ten 2" (5.1cm) lengths of wire. Wrap a 2" (5.1cm) length of wire around one edge of a plain, large oval link on the chain; repeat for each remaining large oval on the chain. Using the flat-nose nylon-jaw pliers, press the wire ends flat.

7. String the 6mm crystals onto individual head pins. Make wrapped loops to attach the beaded head pins in alternating colors to each connector on the chain, except the connectors around and between the focal links (see *Making a Wrapped Loop Dangle* on page 119).

tip

The wrapping pattern is over/under so the beads will be framed inside the flat plane of the oval link. If you consistently wrap over or under on both edges of the link, the beads will raise up on one side of the link.

BRONZE
baubles
necklace

Mixing natural and man-made materials is a big trend in jewelry making, so try your hand at combining leather cord with crystals and wire in unexpected ways. This necklace uses twisted wire for practical and aesthetic reasons. The coils on the sides and ends are making connections, while the twisted rings in the beaded section help bring the look together.

MATERIALS

3 golden shadow 20mm cosmic rings

4 crystal copper 14mm cosmic rings

3 brown pearl 6mm rounds

4 brown pearl 12mm rounds

4 crystal copper 20mm pendants

4 bronze pearl 10mm rounds

4 golden shadow 8mm rounds

8 golden shadow 6mm donuts

4 crystal copper 6mm donuts

4 smoked topaz 8mm rounds

brown polyester chain with 31 links

22-gauge Artistic Wire: nontarnish silver, light brown, brown

brown faux suede lace

4 silver crimp covers

15 silver medium ball head pins

16 silver 5mm spacers

8 silver 8mm jump rings

3 silver 10mm jump rings

TOOLS

jump ring maker with 6mm and 10mm mandrels

wire-twisting tool

hammer and bench block

round-nose pliers

chain-nose pliers

wire cutters

Designer Mighty Crimper

1. Cut a 1-yard (91.4cm) length of each color of wire and attach it to the wire-twisting tool (see *Making Twisted Wire* on page 121). Use the twisted wire with the 10mm mandrel to make 3 complete rings (see *Making Jump Rings* on page 122). Cut the 10mm rings apart and strike them with a hammer to flatten them.

2. Coil the remaining twisted wire on the 6mm mandrel. Cut the 6mm coil into ½" (1.3cm) lengths.

(steps continue on next page) »

3

4

5

6

7

tip

Use this technique to turn your favorite charm bracelet into a necklace.

3. Cut two 10" (25.4cm) lengths of leather cord and pass 1 piece through the last link on each end of the polyester chain.

4. On one side of the necklace, hold the cords as one and pass them through a coil. Slide the coil close to the polyester chain, then tighten the last ring on the coil to hold it in place. Repeat for the other cord.

5. Use a 10mm jump ring to attach a twisted jump ring in front of a golden shadow ring. String a 6mm brown pearl onto a head pin and make a wrapped loop to attach it to the same jump ring (see *Making a Wrapped Loop Dangle* on page 119).

6. Connect the jump ring to the center link on the chain. Repeat Step 5 to make 2 more matching units. Attach them to links 8 and 24.

7. Make wrapped loop dangles from the following beads and silver head pins and place them on the links specified below:

4 dangles using a 12mm brown pearl, silver spacer and an 8mm golden shadow round. Attach 1 dangle to links 2, 10, 18 and 24.

4 dangles using 6mm golden shadow donut, silver spacer, 10mm bronze pearl, silver spacer, 6mm golden shadow donut. Attach 1 dangle to links 4, 12, 20 and 28.

4 dangles using the 8mm smoked topaz, silver spacer and a 6mm crystal copper donut. Attach 1 dangle to links 6, 14, 22 and 30.

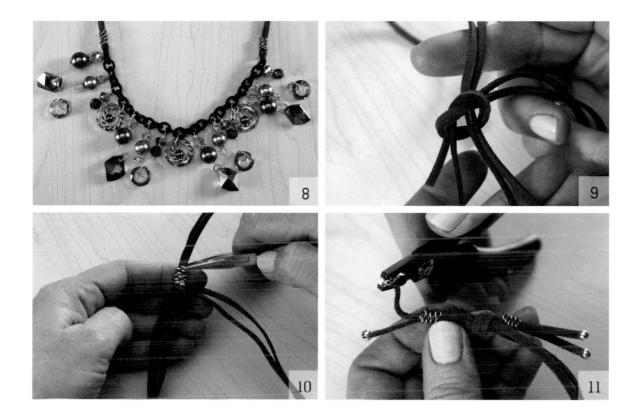

8. Attach 8mm jump rings to the crystal copper pendants and rings. Attach them to the chain as follows: 3 pendant; 5 ring; 11 pendant; 13 ring; 19 pendant; 21 ring; 27 pendant; 29 ring.

9. On one side of the necklace, tie the cords around the opposite end in an adjustable knot. Repeat for the other cord.

10. Pass the short cord ends through a coil and tighten the last ring on the coil to hold it in place. Repeat for the other end.

11. Attach a crimp cover to each cut cord end.

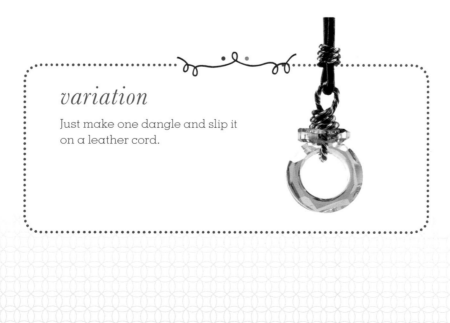

variation

Just make one dangle and slip it on a leather cord.

emerald
CHAIN MAILLE
earrings

As a wireworker, you should give chain maille a try. There are a lot of different weaves, and, of course, whole books are dedicated to the topic. These earrings use parallel (or Helms) weave. It's a fun introductory project because the weave is forgiving enough that you can make your own rings and they're almost instant gratification.

MATERIALS

2 emerald 10mm crystal bicones

2 crystal golden shadow 6mm crystal rondelles

18-gauge Artistic Wire: nontarnish brass, nontarnish silver

2 silver medium ball head pins

TOOLS

round-nose pliers

chain-nose pliers

wire cutters

nylon hammer and bench block

wire jig with small and large pegs

jump ring maker with 6, 8 and 10mm mandrels

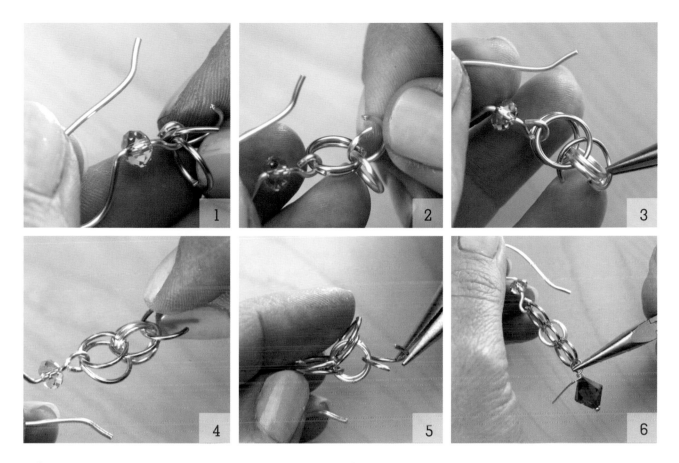

1. Use the jump ring maker to make eight 8mm bronze rings, two 10mm bronze rings, and four 6mm silver rings (see *Making Jump Rings* on page 122). Use silver wire and a crystal golden shadow rondelle to make an ear wire (see *Making an Ear Wire* on page 123). Attach 2 bronze 8mm rings to the lower loop on an ear wire

2. Attach 2 silver 6mm rings side by side on the bronze rings.

3. Pass a 10mm bronze ring around the outside of the 2 silver rings, sandwiching it between the first 2 bronze rings.

4. Pass an 8mm bronze ring through the silver rings and over the edge of the 10mm bronze ring.

5. Attach a bronze ring to the back of the same section.

6. Pass a head pin through a bicone and make a wrapped loop to attach it to the lowest set of rings (see *Making a Wrapped Loop Dangle* on page 119)

Repeat Steps 1–6 to make a matching earring.

variation

Chain maille works best when the aspect ratios of the rings are perfectly matched to the type of weave you want to do. It takes a little bit of experimenting when you make your own rings, so earrings are a perfect starter project. For a smaller version of the chain maille earrings, use 5mm–7mm rings with 6mm × 9mm crystal teardrops.

MOSSY copper bracelet

This sparkly bracelet starts with a handmade, split-ring chain. If you like the look of plain wire chain, you could leave it as is. Or add crystals on beading wire to increase the sparkle factor.

MATERIALS

55 crystal copper 6mm rondelles

55 erinite 6mm rondelles

18-gauge Artistic Wire: brown, natural (light brown)

0.018" (0.5mm) diameter satin copper 19-strand beading wire

2 copper no. 1 crimp tubes

TOOLS

jump ring maker with 8mm mandrel

chain-nose pliers

round-nose pliers (optional)

wire cutters

1. Using the 8mm mandrel, make 3" (7.6cm) wire coils using the brown and natural wires. Remove the coil from the mandrel and count down 3 complete spirals. Separate the section from the main coil and cut.

2. Using the chain-nose pliers, slightly turn in the cut ends to the inner portion of the coil. Repeat Steps 1–2 until you have 12 brown and 12 natural spiral sections.

3. To connect the coils, start with 1 brown and 1 natural colored coil. Lift the wire end and thread it onto the other coil. Twist the coil until it is fully wound onto the other coil.

4. Continue attaching the coils, alternating the brown and natural coils, until all the coils are used.

5. Cut a 28" (71.1cm) length of 19-strand beading wire. At one end of the split-ring chain, thread the wire and center it in the link.

6. On one side of the wire, add 5 copper rondelles. Add 5 erindite rondelles to the other side. Skip the perpendicular link and pass the wire ends through the next split ring.

7. Repeat Step 6, adding the same color beads to the same ends of the wire.

8. Repeat Steps 6–7 until you've used all the beads and have reached the end of the split-ring chain. Crimp the ends of the wire with a crimp tube (see *Using Crimp Beads* on page 117). Trim the excess wire.

9. Use an 18" (45.7cm) length of the brown wire to make a hook (see *Making a Hook* on page 120). Connect the hook by threading its loop through the end split ring.

STREET SMART *necklace*

This is one of my favorite necklaces because it uses a variety of techniques and it goes with almost any outfit. Wire embellishments make it uniquely yours.

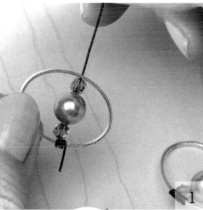

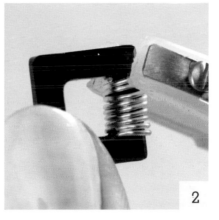

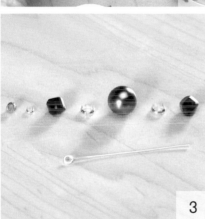

1. Cut a 4" (10.2cm) length of black wire. Wrap it 6 to 8 times around the edge of an oval link, just slightly above the center. Pass the wire through a 4mm black diamond, 8mm light grey pearl and a 4mm black diamond. Wrap the wire around the opposite edge of the oval as shown. Repeat for 7 more oval links.

2. Cut four 5" (12.7cm) lengths of silver wire. Wrap a piece of wire around one side of a square ring. Trim the ends so the cut wire is snug against the inner edge of the ring. Repeat for 3 square rings.

3. Pass an eye pin through: 4mm black diamond, 4mm rondelle, 8mm jet, 6mm rondelle, 12mm dark grey pearl, 6mm rondelle, 8mm jet, 4mm rondelle, 4mm black diamond. Repeat for 3 more eye pins.

(steps continue on next page) »

MATERIALS

24 black diamond 4mm rounds

10 black diamond 6mm rounds

12 light grey opal 6mm rounds

12 jet 6mm helixes

10 dark grey pearl 6mm rounds

8 light grey pearl 8mm rounds

8 jet 8mm helixes

4 dark grey pearl 12mm rounds

4 jet 14mm cosmic square rings

24-gauge black Artistic Wire

22-gauge nontarnish silver Artistic Wire

38" (96.5cm) silver unsoldered rolo cable chain cut in the following lengths: two 1" (2.5cm) (11 links long each) sections; two 6½" (16.5cm) sections; and two 11½" (29.2cm) sections

8 silver 4mm rondelles

8 silver 6mm rondelles

4 silver 18mm × 25mm oval links

44 silver head pins

4 silver eye pins

8 silver 8mm jump rings

TOOLS

round-nose pliers

chain-nose pliers

wire cutters

flat-nose nylon jaw pliers

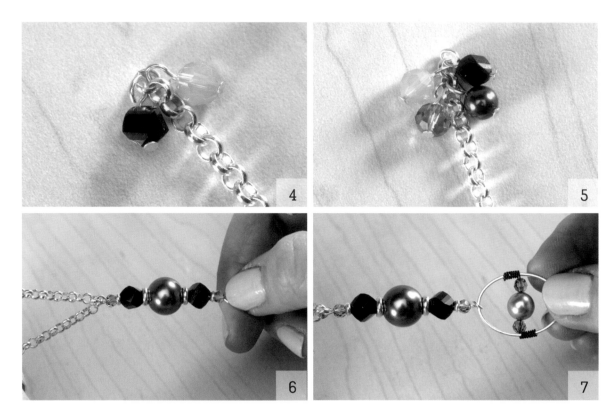

4. String each of the following beads onto individual head pins: 6mm black diamond, 6mm jet, 6mm light grey opal, 6mm dark grey pearl. Make a basic loop on each and cut off any extra wire (see *Making a Basic Loop and Bead Link* on page 118).

   Connect the beads to the 1" (2.5cm) rolo cable chain sections in an alternating pattern. Add a jet on one side of a link and a light grey opal on the other side of the link.

5. On one side of the next link, connect a black diamond and then a dark grey pearl on the other side of the link. Continue alternating pairs of jet/light grey opal and black diamond/dark grey pearl until all 11 links on the chain have dangles. Make another 1" (2.5cm) length of beaded chain.

6. Hold the 6½" (16.5cm) lengths of rolo cable chain together as one and connect a beaded eye pin to one end.

7. Connect an embellished oval to the other end of the same eye pin.

tip

If you feel overwhelmed by the idea of adding all the round dangles to the 1" (2.5cm) chain before constructing the necklace, do the following: Add the plain 1" (2.5cm) chain sections unadorned in Step 10, then add the dangles after you've finished the necklace.

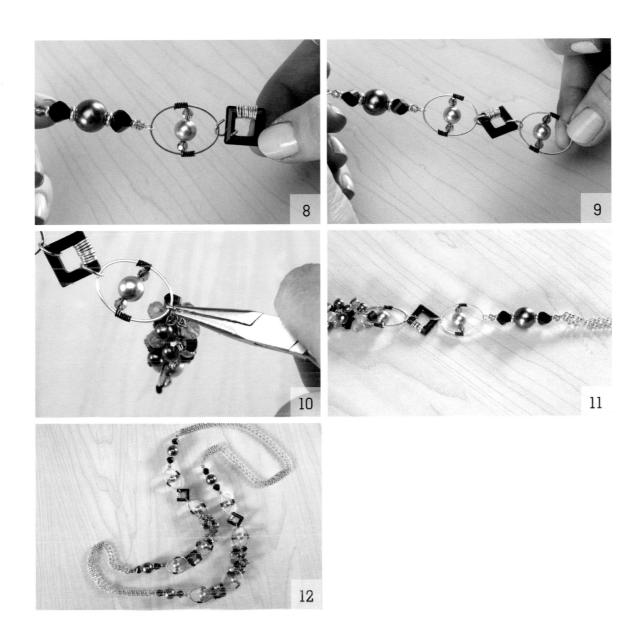

8. Use a jump ring to connect a square ring to the embellished oval.

9. Use another jump ring to attach an embellished oval to the other end of the same square ring.

10. Open the first link on a 1" (2.5cm) length of beaded chain and attach it to the oval.

11. Open the last link on the chain and attach it to another embellished oval. Use a jump ring to connect a square ring to the embellished oval. Use another jump ring to attach an embellished oval to the other end of the same square ring. Connect a beaded eye pin to the last embellished oval. Hold two 11½" (29.2cm) chain lengths together as one and attach them to the other end of the beaded eye pin.

12. Repeat the pattern established in Steps 6–11 to connect the remaining components so the necklace is symmetrical.

JET-SETTER
bangles

Transform ordinary bangle bracelets into stylish statement pieces with layers of wire and crystals. This simple technique is versatile enough to spice up everything from store-bought headbands to plain donut pendants. Use this wrapping pattern to create an encrusted look that also looks neat and finished. Wrap the wire in sections to avoid breakage.

MATERIALS

46 black diamond 4mm rounds

88 jet AB 4mm rounds

22-gauge black Artistic Wire

½" (1.3cm) black plastic bangle bracelet

TOOLS

chain-nose pliers

wire cutters

flat-nose nylon jaw pliers

1. Cut a 2-yard (1.8m) length of wire. Hold the wire end against the inside of the bangle and wrap it 3 times around the bracelet.

   Thread on 3 jet beads, hold them snugly against the outside of the bangle and wrap the wire 3 times around the bracelet so the beaded portions are at least ⅜" (1cm) apart.

2. Repeat the pattern from Step 1 to cover one third of the bracelet.

3. Begin wrapping the wire in the opposite direction, crossing over the beaded wire. Add a jet bead and wrap the wire around the bracelet.

4. Continue wrapping the wire around the bracelet, adding a bead or two on each pass to cover the exposed sections, randomly selecting jet or black diamond beads. The beads should nestle snugly between the triple-beaded wires.

   After reaching the end of the section, reverse direction and wrap a third time with the plain wire. Where needed, fill in with beads.

5. To weave in the wire ends, you need at least a 2" (5.1cm) section. Wrap the wire tightly 3 times around the bangle. Use the chain-nose pliers to tuck the wire tail in and under the wire wraps.

   Use the nylon jaw pliers to press the wires against the inside of the bracelet.

6. You can stop here or repeat the previous steps to cover the remainder of the bracelet.

tip

Too much wire on the inside of the bracelet will affect the fit, so keep your wrapping tidy.

BLACK
diamond
bib necklace

Black diamond is one of my favorite crystal colors. Combine it with clear aurora borealis crystals and the look is absolutely glamorous! I worked on this necklace for quite a while before my *Bead & Wire Jewelry Exposed* co-authors Fernando Dasilva and Margot Potter inspired me to use wire wrapping to add the big, blingy crystals inside the rings. Thank goodness they did! It turned out to be just what the design needed to take it to the next level.

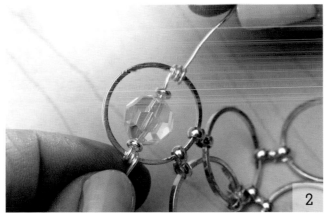

MATERIALS

14 light grey 4mm pearls

38 black diamond 6mm rounds

14 crystal AB 8mm rondelles

5 crystal AB 10mm rounds

1 crystal AB 24mm De-Art pendant

10 silver 3.4mm rondelles

28 silver 6mm beaded rings

20-gauge nontarnish silver Artistic Wire

0.018" (0.5mm) diameter silver 19-strand beading wire

1 silver toggle EZ-Crimp Clasp

2 silver Scrimp findings

2 silver Wire Guardians

10 silver ball-and-star head pins

15 silver 20mm Quick Links rings 30 connectors

TOOLS

round-nose pliers

chain-nose pliers

wire cutters

flat-nose nylon jaw pliers

EZ-Crimp pliers or Designer Mighty Crimper

miniature screwdriver

1. Use the chain-nose pliers to open both sides of a metal connector; repeat for all of the connectors (see *Using Connectors* on page 116). Connect the following number of rings: 5, 4, 3, 2. Now, connect the rows together as shown. Connect a single ring at the bottom of the triangle.

2. Cut a 4" (10.2cm) length of 20-gauge wire and wrap it around the upper left ring, pass it through a 3.4mm rondelle, 10mm round and another 3.4mm rondelle and wrap it around the opposite side of the ring.

(steps continue on next page) »

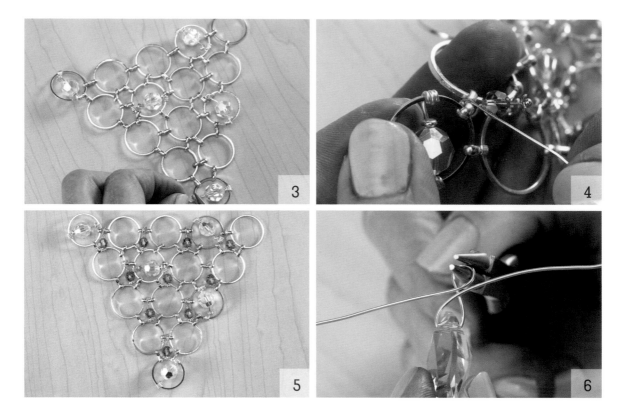

3. Repeat Step 2 for the fourth ring on the top row, second ring on the second row, third ring on the third row and lowest ring on the triangle.

4. String a black diamond onto a head pin and make a wrapped loop to attach it to the first connector on the top row (see *Making a Wrapped Loop Dangle* on page 119).

5. Attach a black diamond head pin to each horizontal connector as shown.

6. Cut a 6" (15.2cm) length of 20-gauge wire and center it through the De-Art pendant. Use the round-nose pliers to bend a loop into one of the wire ends as shown.

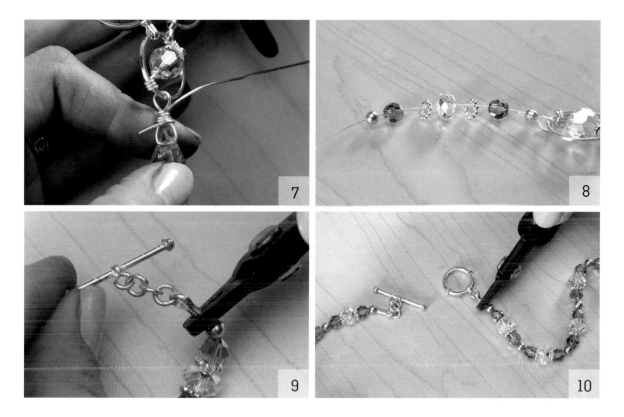

7. Make a wrapped loop to attach the pendant to the lowest ring on the triangle. Trim the excess wire.

8. Cut a 7" (17.8cm) length of beading wire and pass it through a Scrimp finding, Wire Guardian and the outer ring on the first row of links. Secure the wire end in the Scrimp (see *Using Scrimp Findings* on page 116). Pass the wire through the following: black diamond, silver ring, 8mm rondelle, silver ring, black diamond, pearl. Repeat this pattern 6 more times.

9. Trim the wire end to ¼" (6mm) if necessary and pass it inside an EZ Crimp Clasp. Squeeze the finding to close it.

10. Repeat Steps 8–9 for the other side of the necklace, adding the other half of the clasp.

TWISTED
treasure
necklace

This was one of the very first projects I made for this book. I created it to reflect the book's message of combining wirework with other conventional beading techniques to create striking, fashionable jewelry. The twisted jump ring chain always attracts a lot of comments. I made jump rings instead of split rings to make it easier to attach the dangles, but you could certainly substitute split rings if you prefer.

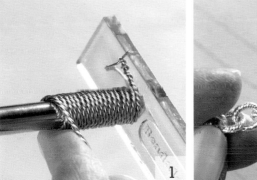

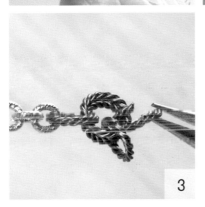

MATERIALS

1 Katiedids 35mm double circle pendant

14 crystal AB 4mm crystal rounds

23 Pacific opal 4mm crystal rounds

10 indicolite 5mm crystal bicones

4 crystal AB 6mm crystal cubes

6 crystal moonlight 6mm crystal bicones

6 light grey opal 6mm crystal rounds

6 crystal 8mm channels

1 indicolite 8mm round

6 indicolite 6mm × 9mm crystal teardrops

2 crystal 18mm twist crystal beads

2 crystal 19mm galactic crystal pendants

20-gauge peacock blue Artistic Wire

22-gauge ice blue Artistic Wire

1 silver interchangeable pendant bail

silver cable chain: medium patterned (two 5 [12.7cm] lengths) and small (twelve 1¼ [3.2cm] lengths)

0.015 (0.4mm) diameter silver 19-strand beading wire

4 silver 6mm solid beaded rings

silver jump rings: four 6mm, two 10mm

silver toggle clasp

TOOLS

round-nose pliers

chain-nose pliers

wire cutters

jump ring maker with 8mm mandrel

wire twisting tool

ruler

1. Cut three 2-yard (1.8m) lengths of the peacock blue wire. Use the wire-twisting tool to twist the wire together (see *Making Twisted Wire* on page 121). Using the 8mm mandrel, make 40 jump rings (see *Making Jump Rings* on page 122).

   Using untwisted blue wire, make six 4mm coils, each ⅝" (1.6cm) in length.

2. Thread 1 twisted jump ring through the end link of the 5" (12.7cm) silver chain. Add 2 more twisted jump rings and close the single jump ring.

3. Open 2 jump rings and thread them through the 2 jump rings attached to the chain.

(steps continue on next page) »

4. Continue connecting the twisted jump rings in pairs. Thread the remaining single jump ring through the end link on the other 5" (12.7cm) silver chain.

5. Pass a head pin through an 8mm indicolite round and through the holes on the double circle pendant. Make a wrapped loop to attach it to the interchangeable pendant bail (see *Making a Wrapped Loop Dangle* on page 119).

6. Cut a 6" (15.2cm) piece of beading wire and pass it under the head pin inside the small channel on the pendant. Pass through 14 crystal AB 4mm rounds.

7. Pass the wire ends through opposite sides of the last few beads. Press the beaded circle down into the channel. Cut off any extra beading wire. Repeat Steps 6–7 to string 23 Pacific opal rounds in the outer channel.

8. Locate the center of the jump ring chain and attach the pendant.

9

10

11

9. For the dangles, make the following:

   Two: 8mm clear channel on 4mm jump ring

   Two: 6mm light grey opal round, silver rondelle, 6mm crystal AB cube on head pin

   Six: 6mm crystal moonlight, ice blue coil, 5mm indicolite bicone, 1¼" (3.2cm) chain on head pin

   Four: 8mm clear channel on eye pin, 5mm indicolite bicone (attach jump ring on two of the dangles)

   Two: 6mm × 9mm indicolite teardrop on head pin

   Two: 18mm twist crystal bead on head pin with 1¼" (3.2cm) chain

   Two: 19mm galactic pendant, 10mm jump ring, 1¼" (3.2cm) length of chain

   Two: 6mm × 9mm indicolite teardrop, silver spacer, 6mm light grey opal round on head pin

   Two: 6mm × 9mm indicolite teardrop on head pin, 6mm crystal cube on head pin, both attached to eye pin. String on 6mm light grey opal round.

10. On both sides of the pendant, attach the following dangles equally spaced apart, on 2 jump rings:

   Two: 18mm twist crystal bead on head pin with 1¼" (3.2cm) chain

   Two: 19mm galactic pendant, 10mm jump ring, 1¼" (3.2cm) length of chain

11. Fill in the necklace with the remaining dangles, matching them on each side.

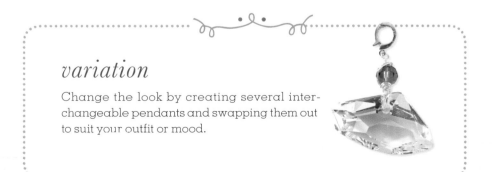

variation

Change the look by creating several interchangeable pendants and swapping them out to suit your outfit or mood.

techniques

One of my favorite things about making jewelry is that it's a pretty portable hobby. You can easily put a little kit together and make beautiful jewelry almost anywhere. These are some of the beading and wirework techniques that I use repeatedly in my work and in the projects for this book. Wrapped loop dangles, bundled wire beads and embellished ear wires are especially easy to make on the go.

general beading techniques

USING CONNECTORS

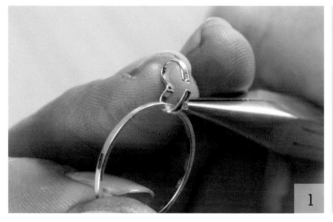 

1. Use the chain-nose pliers to open one side of the connector and place a ring inside. Grasp the end or squeeze it shut with the chain-nose pliers to hold the ring in place.

2. To link 2 rings together, place another ring on the other side of the connector.

USING SCRIMP FINDINGS

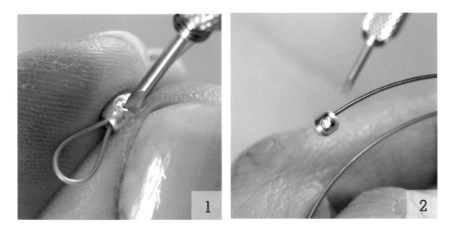

1. Use a miniature screwdriver to loosen the screw inside the finding, pass the wire into the finding, then tighten the screw back again.

2. To use on memory wire, simply loosen the screw, slide the bead onto the end of the wire and tighten the screw.

These are very secure but can be made absolutely permanent with a drop of cyanoacrylate glue.

USING CRIMP BEADS

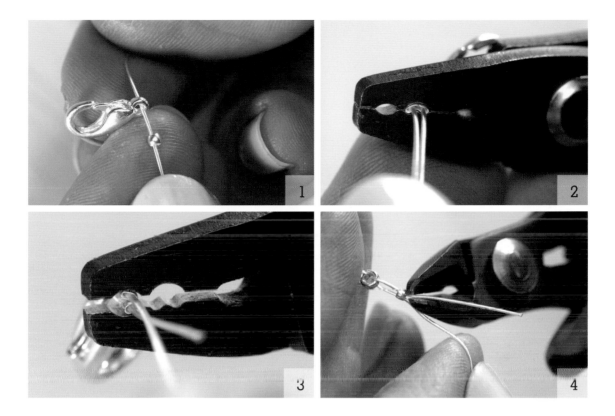

1. Pass the beading wire through the clasp loop and the crimp bead.

2. Thread the wire end back through the crimp bead and squeeze it in the inner jaws of the Designer Mighty Crimper to make a crease.

3. Turn the crimp bead around and place it in the outer jaws. Squeeze gently to fold it.

4. Use wire cutters to cut off the extra wire.

general wirework techniques

MAKING A BUNDLED WIRE BEAD

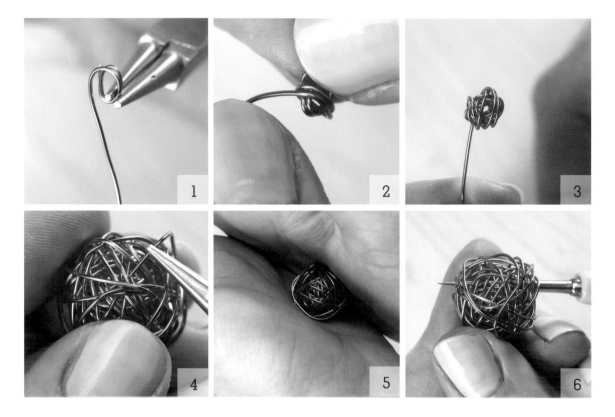

1. Use the round-nose pliers to make an oval shape.

2. Use your fingers to wrap the wire across the oval.

3. Turn the oval and wrap across it from a different direction. Continue wrapping and turning until the bundle is satisfactory.

4. When you get to the last 1" (2.5cm) of wire, use the pliers to turn the wire to a 90-degree angle and stick the wire end into the wire ball.

5. Hold the wire ball between your palms like a lump of clay and rub your hands together to tighten the ball.

6. Use a beading awl to create a hole through the center of the wire ball.

MAKING A BASIC LOOP AND BEAD LINK

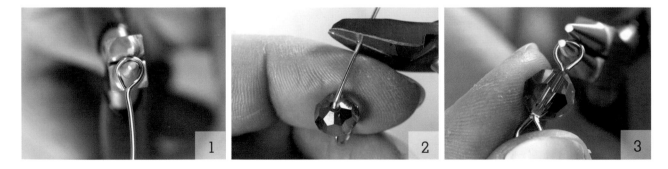

1. For a basic loop, use the round-nose pliers to turn a loop.

2. For a basic loop bead link, add a bead to the wire, then bend the wire in a right angle directly above the bead. Trim the wire to a finger's width.

3. Use the round-nose pliers to turn the wire in a loop.

MAKING A WRAPPED LINK CHAIN

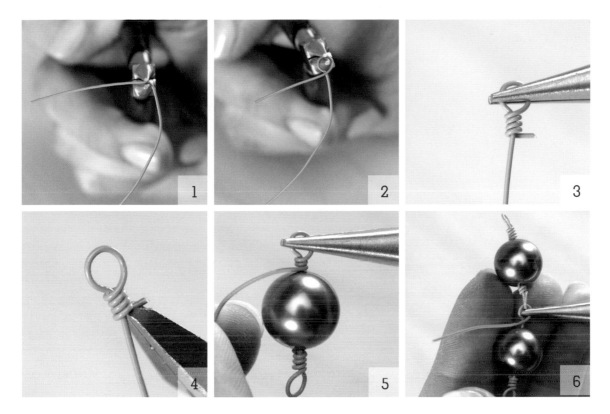

1. Use the chain-nose pliers to make a right angle.
2. Use the round-nose pliers to turn the wire in a loop.
3. Coil the extra wire around the base of the loop.
4. Cut off any extra wire. (It's easier to cut off the wire than to coil the end very tightly. Pressing with pliers can cause the color to chip off.)

5. Add a bead, then make another wrapped loop.
6. When linking beads together, slip the loop onto the previous link before wrapping it shut.

MAKING A WRAPPED LOOP DANGLE

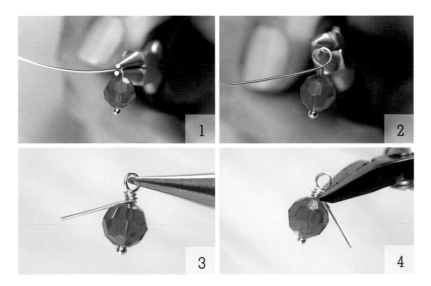

1. Bend the wire in a right angle about ⅛" (3mm) above the bead.
2. Use the round-nose pliers to turn a loop.
3. Coil the extra wire 3 to 4 times around the base of the loop.
4. Cut off any extra wire.

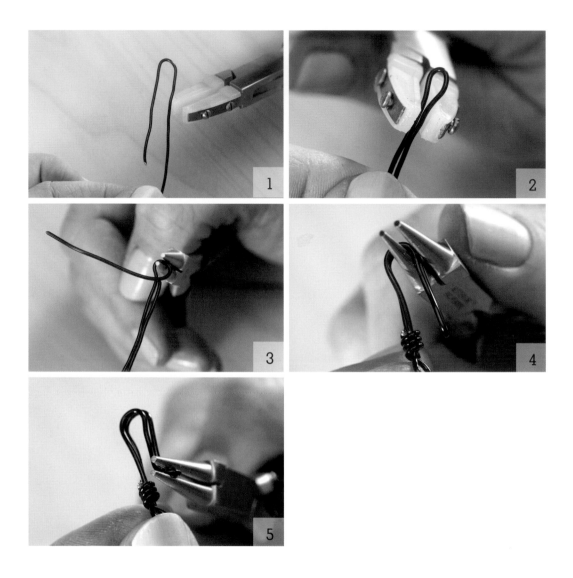

1. To make a hook, use an 18-gauge wire. Cut an 18" (45.7cm) length. Fold the wire back by 1½" (3.8cm).

2. Using the nylon jaw pliers, squeeze the bend in the wire closer together so the doubled wires are parallel.

3. At the end of the doubled wires, bend the single wire in a right angle, then make a wrapped loop.

4. Using the round-nose pliers, bend the doubled portion of wire to create a hook.

5. Use the round-nose pliers to turn up the hook about ¼" (6mm) from the bent end.

USING A COILING GIZMO

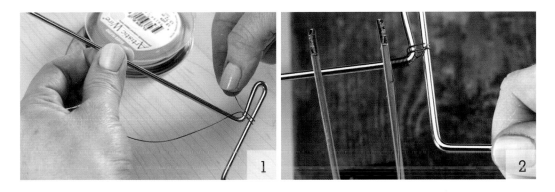

1. Leaving the wire on the spool, wrap the end of the wire around the mandrel as shown.
2. Place the mandrel in a hole on the bracket and turn the handle. Use your nondominant hand to maintain even tension on the wire as it feeds onto the mandrel for a tight, consistent coil.

MAKING TWISTED WIRE

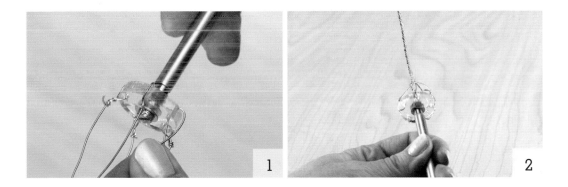

1. To attach each wire to the twisting tool, pass it through a hole on the acrylic plate. Wrap it around the edge of the plate and coil it several times around itself.
2. Attach the other end of the wires to a secure surface such as a clamp or doorknob. Keep the wire ends as even as possible to ensure a clean twist. Turn the handle to twist the wires, continuing until the wire breaks off and is completely work hardenend.

USING A JUMP RING MAKER

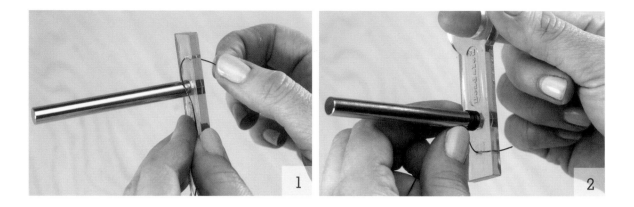

1. Leaving the wire on the spool, feed the wire end through the small hole on the acrylic plate.

2. Use your dominant hand to turn the acrylic handle as your nondominant hand guides the wire onto the mandrel.

MAKING JUMP RINGS

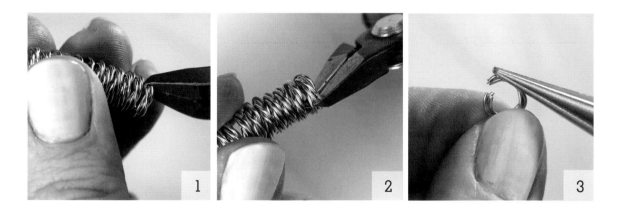

1. Start by using a Coiling Gizmo or a jump ring maker or making a coil by hand. Use flush cutters to cut the first ring off the coil.

2. Trim the other end of the ring, turning the wire cutters so the flat side of the blades touches the end. This way, the ends will fit snugly together.

3. Always open jump rings by turning one end to the side. Never pull the ends directly apart. When you close a ring, push one end past the other until you hear a *click*, then bring the ends back even with each other.

MAKING AN EAR WIRE

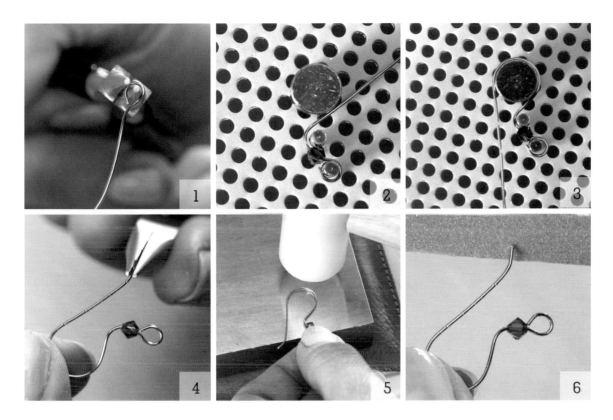

1. Cut a 2" (5.1cm) piece of wire and make a small loop on one end.
2. Pass it through a 4mm crystal and press the loop onto a small peg on the jig.
3. Bend the wire around a large peg on the jig.

4. Remove the ear wire from the jig and trim the end. Use the chain-nose pliers to "kick out" the end in a short, sharp bend.
5. Flatten the ear wire with a hammer and bench block.
6. Use an emery board or file to smooth the end of the ear wire.

EMBELLISHING AN EAR WIRE

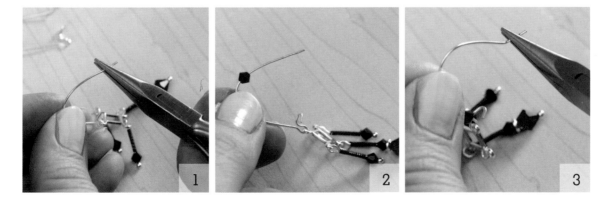

1. Use the chain-nose pliers to straighten the end of an ear wire.
2. Slide a bead onto the ear wire. If desired, hold the bead in place with coiled wire or Bead Bumpers.

3. Bend the end of the ear wire back to its original position.

index

dedication

Live Wire Jewelry is dedicated to my children, Lily and Parker, who enjoy a little creative chaos. Lucky me!

acknowledgments

You've heard that phrase "It takes a village to raise a child"? Well, the same could be said for this book, which I wrote with the help of many friends, family members and colleagues. My husband, Craig, gets a gold star for life. I'm also especially grateful to our parents, who are always there for us, and to my friend and studio assistant, Nikia Bradley, whose enthusiasm is absolutely contagious.

Thanks to the teams at Beadalon and Swarovski North America for believing in my work and providing the materials for this book. Thanks also to the viewers of *Beads, Baubles & Jewels*, my workshop students near and far, and my blog readers for encouraging me to keep the ideas flowing. I feel incredibly lucky to do this creative job for a living, and one of the best parts is the friends I've made along the way. You inspire me, lift me up and make me laugh. Thank you!

Thanks to the whole North Light team, with special gratitude to editor Rachel Scheller for carefully reading the book and taking the reins; editor Julie Hollyday and photographer Christine Polomsky for great step-by-step photos and a fun week in the photo studio; designer Megan Richards for the stylish cover and book design; photographer Ric Deliantoni and stylist Lauren Emmerling for their skillful contributions; editorial director Christine Doyle and Tonia Davenport for shepherding this book into production; and to all of the people behind the scenes who have contributed to the success of *Live Wire Jewelry*.

about the author

Katie Hacker is an artist and writer who started designing her own jewelry as a teenager when she couldn't find fashionable clip earrings for her unpierced ears. She turned her pastime into a business, making jewelry and sharing her ideas. Katie is the host of the public television series *Beads, Baubles & Jewels*, the top TV source for jewelry-making education and inspiration nationwide. Viewers connect with Katie's approachable style and "you can do it!" attitude. A prolific author, Katie's books have sold more than half-a-million copies and cover a variety of techniques from simple stringing to wire wrapping. Katie's line of Katiedids™ Creative Components manufactured by Beadalon gives beaders the power to completely customize their designs. Read Katie's popular beading blog at www.KatieHacker.com.

www.fwmedia.com

16   15   14   13   12   5   4   3   2   1

DISTRIBUTED IN CANADA BY FRASER DIRECT

100 Armstrong Avenue

Georgetown, ON, Canada L7G 5S4

Tel: (905) 877-4411

DISTRIBUTED IN THE U.K. AND EUROPE BY F&W MEDIA INTERNATIONAL

Brunel House, Newton Abbot, Devon, TQ12 4PU, England

Tel: (+44) 1626 323200, Fax: (+44) 1626 323319

Email: enquiries@fwmedia.com

DISTRIBUTED IN AUSTRALIA BY CAPRICORN LINK

P.O. Box 704, S. Windsor NSW, 2756 Australia

Tel: (02) 4577-3555

SRN: X9676

ISBN 13: 978-1-4403-1278-6

Edited by Julie Hollyday and Rachel Scheller
Designed by Megan Richards
Production coordinated by Greg Nock
Photography by Christine Polomsky and Ric Deliantoni
Styling by Lauren Emmerling

METRIC CONVERSION CHART		
To convert	*to*	*multiply by*
Inches	Centimeters	2.54
Centimeters	Inches	0.4
Feet	Centimeters	30.5
Centimeters	Feet	0.03
Yards	Meters	0.9
Meters	Yards	1.1